FIVE YEARS AHEAD OF MY TIME

The REVERB series looks at the connections between music, artists and performers, musical cultures and places. It explores how our cultural and historical understanding of times and places may help us to appreciate a wide variety of music, and vice versa.

reverb-series.co.uk
SERIES EDITOR: JOHN SCANLAN

Already published

The Beatles in Hamburg
IAN INGLIS

Brazilian Jive: From Samba to Bossa and Rap
DAVID TREECE

Easy Riders, Rolling Stones: On the Road in America, from Delta Blues to '70s Rock
JOHN SCANLAN

Gypsy Music: The Balkans and Beyond
ALAN ASHTON-SMITH

Five Years Ahead of My Time: Garage Rock from the 1950s to the Present
SETH BOVEY

Heroes: David Bowie and Berlin
TOBIAS RÜTHER

Jimi Hendrix: Soundscapes
MARIE-PAULE MACDONALD

Neil Young: American Traveller
MARTIN HALLIWELL

Nick Drake: Dreaming England
NATHAN WISEMAN-TROWSE

Peter Gabriel: Global Citizen
PAUL HEGARTY

Remixology: Tracing the Dub Diaspora
PAUL SULLIVAN

Sting: From Northern Skies to Fields of Gold
PAUL CARR

Tango: Sex and Rhythm of the City
MIKE GONZALEZ AND MARIANELLA YANES

Van Halen: Exuberant California, Zen Rock'n'roll
JOHN SCANLAN

FiVE YEARS AHEAD OF MY TiME

GARAGE ROCK FROM THE 1950s TO THE PRESENT

SETH BOVEY

REAKTION BOOKS

Dedicated
to all garage bands everywhere

Published by Reaktion Books Ltd
Unit 32, Waterside
44–48 Wharf Road
London N1 7UX, UK
www.reaktionbooks.co.uk

First published 2019
Copyright © Seth Bovey 2019

Printed and bound in Great Britain by Bell & Bain, Glasgow

A catalogue record for this book is available from the British Library
ISBN 978 1 78914 065 1

Contents

Introduction
The Pioneers: Instrumental Rock and the First Garage Combos

The rock 'n' roll craze died down as dramatically as it began, with most big-name performers being silenced or compromised by the end of the 1950s. As early as 1957, Little Richard shocked fans by deciding to leave the music business and enter the ministry. In 1958, Elvis Presley began his two-year hitch in the u.s. army, Gene Vincent lost his house and his band owing to financial difficulties and Jerry Lee Lewis was blacklisted from radio airplay after the press discovered that he had married his thirteen-year-old cousin, Myra Gala Brown. In 1959, a plane crash in Iowa killed Richie Valens, The Big Bopper and Buddy Holly. Chuck Berry was arrested under the Mann Act for transporting a fourteen-year-old girl across state lines for 'immoral purposes' and, in 1960, was tried and convicted. That same year, Eddie Cochran was killed in Britain in a car accident that also severely injured Gene Vincent's leg.

Rock 'n' roll obviously survived these setbacks, but the mix of artists being promoted on Top 40 radio changed. Figures such as Bill Haley, Fats Domino and Bo Diddley continued to perform and produce hit records, but they were overshadowed in the marketplace by a horde of teen idols and white-bread pop singers. The airwaves were crowded with sappy love songs by the likes of Dion, Paul Anka, Bobbie Vee and Frankie Avalon as well as the tame pop numbers of Connie Francis and Pat Boone. Yet this situation was hardly static, for a couple of other developments were taking place at the time. One was the rise of instrumental rock, in which the singing was replaced by melody lines played on the organ, saxophone or guitar. Without lyrics, instrumentalists had to keep the listener's attention by offering a raucous, energetic performance and novel sounds. Thus every 'intro' had to have a gimmick, which could be the tune of a well-known traditional song, intriguing sound effects or vocal noises – shouts, whoops, rebel yells, whistles, laughs, cat-calls – anything to stir up the blood or pique the listener's interest. Instrumentals began appearing around 1957 as hits in the Billboard Top 100, proving that at least some segment of the record-buying public wanted to keep on hearing untamed rock 'n' roll. One of the earliest was Bill Justis's 'Raunchy', a tune that rose to No. 2 in the pop charts by October 1957. 'Raunchy' begins with a string-bending, country-flavoured guitar riff that every guitar player in America wanted to learn after hearing it. The intro is followed by a smooth, dreamy sax melody; underneath, the song is pure rhythm and blues, with a deep horn part that satisfies the soul. Most instrumentals followed the same basic formula, with some featuring wailing sax-ophones, as in 'Walkin' with Mr Lee,' a 1957 hit by Lee Allen, while others were dominated by the organ, such as Dave 'Baby' Cortez's 'The Happy Organ', which was a No. 1 hit in 1959, or Johnny and the Hurricanes' 'Red River Rock', a No. 5 hit. However, the ones with the most lasting impact were guitar-based concoctions, such as Link Wray's 'Rumble', a No. 16 hit in the same year, or Duane Eddy's No. 6 hit in 1958, 'Rebel-Rouser'.[1]

Both Eddy and Wray have risen to 'guitar hero' status because of their innovations in modifying the sound of the electric guitar. Eddy's gimmick was his so-called 'twangy' sound, which was due partly to his technique and partly to sound effects. When Eddy was discovered as a teenager by producer Lee Hazlewood, he was a coun-try musician who naturally had that string-bending country twang in his guitar licks. After being in the studio a few times, Eddy also hit upon the idea of playing melodies on the low strings, mainly because

As rock's first guitar hero, Duane Eddy inspired legions of young guitarists to play, and his 'twangy' sound showed that the guitar could have an expressive voice.

the bass notes 'recorded better' than the treble ones.[2] For his part, Hazlewood was a Phoenix-based DJ who was already experimenting with echo devices, using copious amounts of echo on several songs recorded with guitarist Al Casey.[3] To prepare for Eddy's recordings, Hazlewood rigged up an echo chamber by putting a speaker and a mic in a gigantic, empty water tank; he then ran the sound of Eddy's hollow-body Gretsch guitar through that as well as a DeArmond tremolo unit, which gave it a pulsating or shimmering sound.[4] Eddy tried out his low-pitched, reverberating, string-bending sound on their first 45 rpm single, 'Movin' 'n' Groovin'', which only made it to No. 72 in the charts, but the next one, 'Rebel-Rouser', was a smash hit that stayed in the charts for thirteen weeks.[5] After recording their next couple of hits, 'Ramrod' and 'Cannonball', Eddy and Hazlewood had established their formula for success: a fast guitar boogie/shuffle or country-and-western backing track, over which was laid Eddy's twangy guitar riffs, along with dirty-toned sax solos, echoed handclaps and the excited yelps of vocal group The Sharps. This electrifying combination not only sold records but caused many a youngster to pick up a guitar and try to play like Duane Eddy.[6]

The same kind of emulation was inspired by Link Wray's radical sound. Realizing early on that he wouldn't be able to play like Chet Atkins, Tal Farlow or the other 'jazz cats' he admired, Wray began experimenting with the sound of his guitar, pioneering the use of distortion, power chords and extreme tone settings.[7] All three of these techniques can be heard in 'Rumble', his first hit, which started off as a rough-and-tough tune he made up on the spot when the DJ at a record hop asked Wray and His Ray Men to play something with a stroll beat, a popular rhythm at the time. When the Ray Men recorded 'Rumble' in the studio, Wray thought his 1953 Les Paul guitar and Premier amplifier sounded too clean, so he took a pen and punched holes in the amp's paper tweeter cones,[8] resulting in the shrill, metallic, gritty buzz-saw tone one hears on the record instead of the warm, sweet-sounding distortion one gets from an overdriven tube amp. On top of that, Wray kept turning up the gain on his tremolo unit throughout the song, so that by the end one hears shuddering waves of grungy sound instead of guitar chords. Such effects seem old hat to listeners today, but they must have been a revelation for rock 'n' roll fans in 1958, who had no doubt never heard such a raunchy tone come out of a guitar before. Furthermore, 'Rumble' established the formula for many of Wray's subsequent instrumentals: blues-based riffs and chord progressions played over a walking bass pattern, along with the plunking of a Jerry Lee Lewis-style honky-tonk piano part and Chuck Berry-style guitar licks for solos. Wray plays a combination of barre chords and power chords on this song, sometimes suspending a chord over the beat of the rhythm section instead of strumming along with the beat, and other times strumming along with power chords, which involve playing the lower two or three strings of a barre chord and damping the treble strings to create a heavier sound. Evidently, record buyers liked what they heard, for Wray's follow-up to 'Rumble' was 'Rawhide', and it rose to No. 23 in the charts in 1959. Even though Wray and His Ray Men would never again record a tune as successful as either of these,

Wray became a venerated guitar player; Pete Townshend once wrote: 'He is the king; if it hadn't been for Link Wray and "Rumble", I would have never picked up a guitar.'[9]

The influence of musicians such as Eddy and Wray was enhanced by another development in the late 1950s: the increasing coverage of pop music on television. Many rock 'n' rollers appeared on variety shows such as *The Guy Mitchell Show*, *The Steve Allen Show* and *The Ed Sullivan Show*, reaching a larger public than they could by simply having hit records and touring the dance halls. The teen dance shows had even more impact, and cities such as New York, Baltimore and Washington, DC, had their own such shows on local television

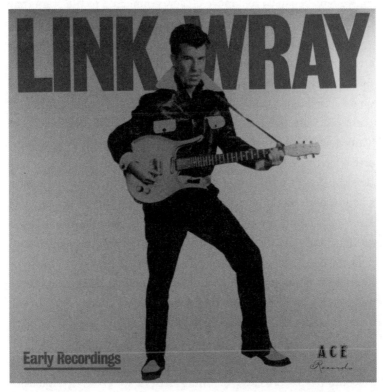

Link Wray could be seen as the second guitar hero of rock, and he gave the guitar's voice even more grain and texture through distorted power chords and extreme tone settings.

stations, but it was Dick Clark's Philadelphia-based *Bandstand* that became the most influential one after ABC began broadcasting it nationwide in August 1957. By February 1958, the renamed *American Bandstand* averaged 8.4 million viewers a day, most of whom were teenagers and housewives, and by January 1959 it was the top daytime show in the country.[10] This show gave viewers throughout America, no matter how remote from the urban centres, a chance to keep up with the latest hit records and dance steps and to see the hit-makers of the day perform. It also allowed them to see the performers interact with Clark, whose easy-going, congenial manner brought the stars down to earth and made them seem familiar; consequently, music fans began to feel more closely connected to the stars than they had through the mediums of radio and fan magazines.

This process of familiarization included the many instrumental artists who appeared on Clark's shows after having hit records in the Billboard charts. For instance, Bill Justis and His Combo appeared on *American Bandstand* in 1957 and on the *Dick Clark Saturday Night Beech-nut Show* in 1958 to play along with their hits 'Raunchy' and 'College Man'. Likewise, Link Wray and His Ray Men were guest artists on the *Saturday Night Beech-nut Show* twice and on *American Bandstand* once to promote 'Rumble' and 'Rawhide'. More impressively, Duane Eddy performed nine times on the *Saturday Night Beech-nut Show* from 1958 to 1960 and a whopping seventeen times on *American Bandstand* from 1958 to 1966.[11] However, these numbers seem less striking after one finds out that Clark had a financial interest in Jamie Records, Duane Eddy's Philadelphia-based label, and that he was promoting Eddy to make more money for himself, a practice that Clark had to answer for when he testified before a Congressional subcommittee during the Payola hearings of 1960.[12] Setting aside the issue of Clark's ethics, the point here is that his promotion of records and recording artists also served to popularize the idea of being in a musical group and playing rock 'n' roll. Viewers could see that Clark's featured guests seemed to enjoy playing their music in front of enthusiastic and appreciative studio audiences. Moreover, the instrumental stars played tunes that were relatively simple and easy to learn; a kid might not have the singing voice of a Dion or Paul Anka, but anyone with basic skills on an instrument could figure out the main parts of 'Raunchy' or 'Rebel-Rouser'. Thus young people throughout the country began entertaining the notion of learning an instrument or forming a rock 'n' roll combo.

A television show of a different kind that encouraged youngsters to play rock 'n' roll was *The Adventures of Ozzie and Harriet*, a sitcom that could be seen as a forerunner of today's reality shows. Ostensibly based on the real-life experiences of the Nelson family, the programme was produced, directed and written by father Ozzie and served as the platform that launched Ricky Nelson's musical career. As a youngster, Ricky took an interest in rock 'n' roll, and when a girlfriend of his had a crush on Elvis, sixteen-year-old Ricky bragged that he was about to cut his own record and called upon his father to make it happen. Ricky then recorded a cover version of Fats Domino's 'I'm Walkin'' while Ozzie produced an episode called 'Ricky the Drummer', which featured Ricky singing the song at a local dance; this episode aired in April 1957 – the same week that Ricky's single was released. The record sold 1 million copies in the first week, and for the next six years Ricky had a string of hits in the charts.[13] As a teen heartthrob, he had charisma and the pretty-boy looks of Elvis, but he was a nice, well-scrubbed boy from an upmarket neighbourhood as opposed to a working-class Southerner. Indeed, Ricky's non-threatening persona, along with Ozzie and Harriet's support for his singing career, helped to convince middle-class Americans that rock 'n' roll was not the Devil's music but an acceptable musical outlet for teenagers.[14] At the same time, Ricky's stupendous success, especially his appeal to girls, gave many teenage boys ideas about what could happen if they were to learn how to sing and play the guitar.

Evidence of the rock 'n' roll trend can be seen in the upswing in the number of amateurs learning to play musical instruments as well as the increase in sales of instruments during the 1950s and '60s. According to music industry reports published in *Billboard* magazine, one in every 7.2 Americans played an instrument in 1950; that number rose to one in every 4.8 by 1966. Among school-age children (ages 4 to 21), 3 million were amateur musicians in 1950; by 1967, that number had risen to 15.4 million, a fivefold increase. Sales of instruments used in rock 'n' roll are especially revealing. In 1956, 200,000 drum sets were sold; ten years later that figure hit 1.1 million. Harmonicas show the same sort of climb, from 400,000 units sold in 1956 to 1 million in 1966.[15] Guitar sales jumped even higher in that same ten-year period, with the number of units sold going up six times; interestingly, this upswing occurred before the Beatles Invasion, with 400,000 guitars being sold in 1962 and 700,000 in 1963. In monetary terms, $23 million was spent on guitars and amplifiers in 1955; by 1966, sales totalled more than $140 million.[16]

Reasons for this jump in popularity vary, but, as Sydney Katz, president of the Kay Musical Instrument Company, stated in the guitar industry report of 1956, 'No matter how you feel about rock 'n' roll and Elvis Presley, for business they have been great, and guitar sales have been rising steadily as a result.'[17] Here, Katz suggests that amateur musicians were little more than imitators of rock 'n' roll stars. In the same report, Charles Rubovits of the Harmony guitar company offers a more nuanced explanation for the rise in sales: 'More people have the desire to do things themselves rather than be spectators; more people have leisure time; more people are more easily exposed to music through television, creating a desire for self-expression; and more people have and will have more money to buy the things they want.'[18] Rubovits's observation about people wanting to play music to express themselves instead of being mere spectators seems particularly insightful, calling attention to the do-it-yourself mentality that Americans had in the mid-twentieth century. Ten years after Rubovits's analysis, the music industry report of 1966 adds a couple of other reasons for rising guitar sales: the influx of cheap Japanese imports and the idea that the guitar is the easiest instrument to learn how to play.[19] These reasons, in addition to the guitar being the main instrument of rock 'n' roll, help to explain why the instrument became so popular.

Naturally, aspiring young guitarists began seeking each other out and learning how to play songs with other like-minded musicians. As a result, homegrown rock 'n' roll combos – which we now refer to as 'garage bands' – began forming throughout America around 1958 or so. These fledgling bands played with more energy and enthusiasm than technical skill, and they have been retroactively tagged with the 'garage' label because they commonly practised in the garage of someone's family home and their sound was often crude and unrefined, much like the unfinished interior of a garage. For such bands to thrive, they had to be surrounded by an infrastructure that could help them develop beyond amateur status. In those days that meant having a healthy population of teens who wanted to dance to rock 'n' roll, along with venues that would be willing to host dances. It also meant having local DJs or businessmen who wanted to get into hosting record hops, managing acts and producing records. Recording could only take place if some kind of recording studio existed, and this was usually a primitive facility in a local radio station, used for recording commercials. Moreover, only a lucky few of these bands were able to connect with a regional record company that was willing to take a chance on a local recording and try to license it to a major record company in the hope of scoring a nationwide hit.

One of the earliest, most precocious, influential and fortunate garage bands from the late 1950s was The Fabulous Wailers, of Tacoma, Washington. Just why such an outstanding band should come out of Tacoma, a seaport and ship-building town south of Seattle, remains a bit of a mystery, but it surely must have had something to do with the kids in the area being so hungry for rock 'n' roll. At any rate, The Wailers started off in 1957 as a jazz band formed by two high-schoolers, acoustic bassist Woody Mortenson and trumpeter John Greek. Billing themselves variously as the MGS, the M-G Trio, the M-G Quartet and so forth, and filling in their line-up with hired players, Mortenson and Greek happened across a promising guitarist named Rich Dangel, whom they paid a pittance to help them do a few rock 'n' roll numbers at sock hops.[20] After realizing that their audience preferred rock 'n' roll to jazz, Greek moved in that direction and the MGS began playing instrumental rock numbers. Soon, the jazz musicians dropped out of the line-up and the band became a New Orleans-style rock 'n' roll combo with piano (Kent Morrill), saxophone (Mark Marush), guitar (Rich Dangel and John Greek) and drums (Mike Burk). Greek renamed them The Nitecaps, and they played their first paying gig at The Snakepit, the enlisted men's club at McChord Air Force Base. After they played some local teen dances, the area's leading dance band, a white rhythm-and-blues outfit called The Blue Notes, asked The Nitecaps to open a dance for them at American Lake. The Nitecaps accepted the offer, changed their name to The Wailers and went down well with The Blue Notes' crowd. Before long, The Wailers were drawing eight hundred kids to their dances while the R&B-oriented Blue Notes were only drawing two hundred, and their appearance at the 1958 All-City Halloween Dance in Tacoma drew 1,800 teenagers.[21] Building on their popularity, the group began putting on their own 'Wailers House Parties', renting the venues and Coca-Cola machines themselves and printing their own posters to advertise the shows.[22]

The Wailers also stayed one step ahead of their peers when it came to writing their own songs, recording and gaining national attention. In August 1958, they went to Commercial Recorders of Seattle and cut an original tune called 'Scotch on the Rocks'. Their manager, a big-band leader from New York named Art Mineo, took the demo tape and shopped it around back east. The interest of Clark Galehouse, owner of Golden Crest Records, was piqued.[23] After Galehouse witnessed one of The Wailers' live shows, he signed the band to a record deal and rushed back to Long Island,

New York, for his state-of-the-art recording gear. He recorded the group live one night in February 1959 after they played a regular gig in the Knights of Columbus Hall in Lakewood, capturing 'Scotch', 'Roadrunner', 'Mau Mau', 'Snakepit' and 'Dirty Robber' on tape. Golden Crest released 'Scotch' as a single after the band gave it the more innocuous title of 'Tall Cool One'. Local teenagers snapped up 20,000 copies within ten days of its release, and during that summer it caught on around the country, rising to No. 45 in the *Cash Box* chart and peaking at No. 36 in the Billboard chart.[24] Listening to it now, one can hear why teenagers found 'Tall Cool One' so thrilling; the intro features Burk playing a jazzy pattern on his hi-hat cymbals while Dangel plays a series of droning power chords. Then Morrill plays some tinkling piano lines and the rest of the band launches into a hard-rocking guitar shuffle, over which Marush blows electrifying sax riffs. With the heavy, full-bodied sound of this tune, The Wailers had taken a big step towards defining the Northwest sound.

To capitalize on their hit song, Golden Crest hurriedly arranged for the band to visit the East Coast. The Wailers bought a new station wagon with their advance money, loaded up their gear in a trailer and drove to New York City. When the boys arrived, they were taken to the top talent agency in America to discuss promotion.[25] This was followed by several trips and television appearances across the u.s. – *The Dick Clark Show* in Philadelphia on 11 June 1959, *The Milt Grant Show* in Washington, DC, *The Buddy Dean Show* in Baltimore and *The Roy Lamont Show* in Richmond – even sharing the bill with Link Wray, their hero, on one show.[26] They also played record hops in Maryland, Virginia, Indiana and Michigan before returning to New York to play the Apollo Theater and to appear on Allen Freed's *Big Beat Show*. In the meantime, Golden Crest had released 'Mau Mau' as the band's follow-up single in June, and it rose to No. 68 in the Billboard chart.[27] The Wailers were headed for the big time, and Golden Crest took them to their studio in July to lay down eight more tracks. The record label then announced their plans to release a Wailers lp, something unheard of for a garage band in those days, but the hitch was that the band needed to relocate to the East Coast so that they could be managed more easily.[28] John Greek was in favour of the move, but most of the other guys, being only sixteen or seventeen years old, were worn out and homesick; they wanted to go home.[29] So back to Tacoma they went, causing a rift between Greek and the band that would eventually result in him being forced from the group.[30]

In spite of Golden Crest's disappointment at having their hot teenage band turn out to be a bunch of mama's boys, they released *The Fabulous Wailers* in March 1960. During an era when very few rock bands released LPS, this record was a real coup for a garage band from the hinterlands. Even though Golden Crest did little to promote the album and sales were low, it represents a huge artistic achievement. The thirteen tunes on the album revealed that The Wailers had great potential for composing and playing instrumental rock. The weakest cut on the LP is the one track with vocals, the Little Richard-inspired 'Dirty Robber'. Piano player Morrill sings

The Wailers in 1959 (left to right: Rich Dangel, Mike Burk, Mark Marush, Kent Morrill, John Greek).

with real gusto, but his high, thin-bodied voice reveals why the group is considered to be a garage combo. Much more impressive are the two jazzy numbers with horns played by Greek: 'Driftwood' is a quiet, Chet Baker-inspired piece, and 'High Walls' is a composition about Devil's Island prison that with its noir-flavoured horn parts sounds as if it came from the soundtrack of a police drama. Several of the rock 'n' roll songs are derivative, with 'Wailin'' echoing Duane Eddy, 'Long Gone' paying homage to Chuck Berry and 'Mau Mau' doing the mambo in the style of 'Tequila', but they are played with exuberance. Three or four of the best tunes, including 'Road Runner', 'Shanghied' and 'Swing Shift', would be called surf music if they had more reverb on the guitars, and the most infectious tunes, 'Tough Bounce' and 'Beat Guitar', have a rhythmic intensity and melodic inventiveness that rival the best rock 'n' roll played by anyone during the 1950s. Despite its low sales, this album had a huge influence on other musicians: The Ventures would later cover four of the tunes from the record, and The Beatles' George Harrison would later claim that he had owned the record 'since day one'.[31] Moreover, *Hit Parader* magazine proclaimed in 1968 that the album was 'the best LP by a white rock instrumental group . . . before the coming of the modern blues and San Francisco scenes'.[32]

Instead of becoming complacent and working the same musical vein after reaching this milestone, The Wailers forged ahead into new musical territory, ironically looking back at the roots of rock 'n' roll by exploring rhythm and blues. They began working with a thirteen-year-old vocal prodigy named Gail Harris, who had the rich, powerful voice of a mature black woman and an obsession with the R&B music of Etta James.[33] The Wailers also inherited a singer from The Blue Notes, a young man who went by the name of Rockin' Robin Roberts. As a record store clerk with a love of Ray Charles, Hank Ballard and the Midnighters, and Richard Berry's 'Louie Louie', Rockin' Robin brought his own R&B obsession to the band.[34] Within the band, guitarist Dangel had been busy studying the tunes of Freddy King, the virtuoso blues guitarist who had jumped onto the instrumental rock bandwagon by releasing *Let's Hide Away and Dance Away with Freddy King* in 1961. More generally, the entire band was hanging out at the Evergreen Ballroom, an R&B club in the Seattle area where performers such as Little Richard, James Brown and Rufus Thomas did their thing.[35] All of this exposure to R&B music caused The Wailers to develop their own version of an R&B revue; a typical set would begin with the ebullient Rockin' Robin singing three or four numbers to get the crowd worked up, and then Gail Harris would sing three or four songs, usually including Etta James's 'All I Could Do Was Cry' and Ike and Tina Turner's 'I Idolize You'. After that, Rockin' Robin and Harris would sing a duet or two. Later, Harris would sing some 'girl group' songs with the Marshans, her three backing singers, and the band would do some instrumentals, including Freddy King's 'San-Ho-Zay' and 'Sen-Say-Shun', in addition to their own material.[36] Because The Wailers had such a large following, these shows played a huge role in popularizing black music among white teenagers in the Pacific Northwest in the early 1960s.

That The Wailers were drawn to black music should not be a surprise. After all, rock 'n' roll was derived directly from post-war rhythm and blues, and the band members were aware of this lineage. They no doubt also had some awareness that

> White popular music has been invigorated by styles and values drawn from black culture – styles and values that lose their original force and meaning as they pass through the bland wringer of mass music but are rediscovered by each new generation of hip musicians and audiences.[37]

Being hipsters, The Wailers naturally gravitated towards what they perceived to be an original, genuine form of musical expression and away from the more commercialized and watered-down imitations of this music heard on pop radio stations. As piano player

Rare & Unreleased From 1961!

Rockin' Robin with the **Fabulous Wailers!!**
PREVIOUSLY UNISSUED STUDIO VERSION OF ROSALIE!!!
EXCLUSIVE INTERVIEW WITH D.C. ON BANDSTAND!!!!

After The Wailers took on vocalists Gail Harris and Rockin' Robin, they moved away from playing instrumental rock to R&B.

Morrill explained in a fairly recent interview: 'I didn't listen to white rock 'n' roll; actually I hated it. I'd hear these guys talking about "Tutti Frutti" by Pat Boone and I'd wanna scream . . . Whom we were not influenced by was guys like Bobby Vinton, all that bubble-gum stuff that was coming along.'[38] Here, we get a glimpse of the disdain that musicians like The Wailers felt for the whitewashed, bowdlerized pop music listened to by bubblegum-popping teeny-boppers as well as a sense of why they wanted to find more authentic forms of musical expression. By searching for authenticity in rhythm and blues, The Wailers hoped to draw substance and vitality from the music of African Americans, who probably seemed to them to draw their music from the wellspring of true musical expression. In general, garage musicians of every period do the same thing: look to the past as some imagined golden age of rock 'n' roll to find authentic material to play, in addition to powerful modes of expression. Yet it would be a mistake to see garage musicians as mere revivalists or purists, for they strive to capture the primal energies of an earlier form of rock 'n' roll instead of merely mimicking it. The riffs, chord progressions, rhythms and lyrical themes that they borrow and which have their origins in rhythm and blues are altered to produce meaning in the youth culture of America.

An example of this process may be seen in the popularization of 'Louie Louie' as a rock 'n' roll dance song. As written and recorded by Richard Berry, 'Louie Louie' began in 1957 as an R&B hit with a cha-cha/calypso beat. By the time The Wailers decided to take it up, 'Louie Louie' was already a standard in the Seattle-area teen scene: the Dave Lewis Combo began playing it in 1957, followed by Ron Holden and the Playboys, The Frantics, The Thunderbirds, The Gallahads and others.[39] Rockin' Robin had even performed it with The Blue Notes,[40] and he began urging The Wailers to record it. The band did so around October 1960, but then they spent the next few months quarrelling over who should get the credits on the single.[41] Meanwhile, the band members also pondered Golden Crest's lack of interest in working with them any further. Rockin' Robin, Morrill and newly acquired bassist Buck Ormsby came up with the idea of forming their own record label; the other three argued against the idea because they didn't want to be limited to regional success.[42] In the end, their hand was forced by the news that The Adventurers and Little Bill Engelhart were about to release their own recording of 'Louie Louie'.[43] Roberts, Morrill and Ormsby acted immediately, ordering copies of The Wailers' single to be pressed up and forming the Etiquette label.

Released in March 1961, The Wailers' single became a local hit, but the best thing that can be said about their recording is that it inspired two up-and-coming garage bands down in Portland, Oregon – Paul Revere and the Raiders and The Kingsmen – to perform and record the song. Of these three versions, The Wailers' is the weakest. Rockin' Robin turns in a spirited vocal performance, but the musicians play as if they are going through the motions. They also play an extra quaver note in the refrain section – left silent in the original – so that the rhythm goes 1-2-3-4 . . . 1-2 instead of 1-2-3 . . . 1-2, causing the song to drag. In addition, Burk's understated drum part is so buried in the mix that the song literally doesn't have a beat, and therefore no forward motion.

Paul Revere and the Raiders' version is by far the most professional sounding of the three. No one has ever sung 'Louie Louie' better than their singer, Mark Lindsey, who has a big, masculine, radio-friendly voice. The instrumental parts are all competently played, but the musicians sit back on the beat and never cut loose; as a result, their take also lacks forward momentum, which is the main thing that The Kingsmen's slop-bucket version has going for it. This recording has the weakest vocal performance of all, with singer Jack Ely slurring the words in his high-pitched, thin-bodied voice, and it is also full of miscues and mistakes. The drummer, for example, hesitates here and there as he thinks about what he should hit next, but his desperate drum-pounding and cymbal-bashing at least propel the song forward, especially in combination with the driving bass lines, so that it has what the other two recordings lack: forward momentum. The deranged guitar solo midway through also gives the song a sense of urgency, and the result is an infectious mess of rock 'n' roll, one that deservedly became the national hit and turned 'Louie Louie' into a frat-rock classic.

Even though The Wailers may have fallen short with their recording of 'Louie Louie', the founding of Etiquette Records by three young, inexperienced members of the band should be seen as a major coup. The label would go on to release eight LPs and 26 singles by such Pacific Northwest garage bands as The Sonics, The Bootmen, The Galaxies, The Rooks and, of course, The Wailers.[44] Thus half of the band became directly involved in producing and promoting garage rock, in essence making them movers and shakers in the Northwest rock scene. To their credit, The Wailers themselves remained a vital garage band for the rest of their decade-long existence. They never achieved nationwide stardom, but they also avoided the fate of so many other garage bands, who ended up as bar bands that played Top 40 covers. In fact, The Wailers continued to grow and develop as a musical group, adapting creatively to the

No song in the canon of garage rock is covered as often as 'Louie Louie', but it is a difficult song to play with the right feel, and no one has done it better than The Kingsmen.

shifts in taste brought on by the British Invasion and the psychedelic movement, and their story serves to illustrate both the possibilities and pitfalls of playing garage rock. Even more significantly, their example shows that the period between the twilight of classic rock 'n' roll and the dawn of Beatlemania was alive with the sounds of garage combos that did their best to keep the Big Beat of rock 'n' roll going when the major record companies were downplaying rock and pushing more sedate and less anarchic forms of pop music.

This magazine ad for Kent guitars capitalizes on one reason that young men
want to learn how to play the guitar – to impress girls.

1

The Founders: American Garage Rock before the Beatles Invasion

T eenagers of the early 1960s were exposed to a wide variety of musical styles, but almost all of them were pop music. A glance at the Billboard charts for 1961 and '62 reveals everything from schmaltzy love songs (Paul Anka's 'Tonight My Love, Tonight') to jazz (Dave Brubeck's 'Take Five'); from white-bread folk (The Highwaymen's 'Cotton Fields') to pop rock (Barry Mann's 'Who Put the Bomp (In the Bomp, Bomp, Bomp)'); from country ballads (Jimmy Dean's 'PT-109') to movie themes (Gene Pitney's 'The Man Who Shot Liberty Valance'); and from nov-elty songs (Ray Stevens's 'Ahab the Arab') to R&B instrumentals (King Curtis's 'Soul Twist'). The charts also teem with songs by the ever-present Elvis, Roy Orbison, Ricky Nelson, Connie Francis and The Everly Brothers. Moreover, numerous hits by The Shirelles ('Will You Love Me Tomorrow' and 'Soldier Boy') signal the begin-ning of the 'girl group' sound that would dominate the pop charts until the British Invasion. Another emerging trend was vocal surf music, as ushered in by The Beach Boys ('Surfin' Safari'), and a con-tinuing trend was the 'dance fad' songs of Chubby Checker ('The Fly' and 'Pony Time'). In spite of this diversity, however, the overall sound of this time was light, clean and smooth, with the prevailing moods being either mawkish and romantic or upbeat and cheery. Music was far more colourful at the regional level, where music fans were offered such delights as Chan Romero's down-and-dirty rockabilly number 'My Little Ruby', Fat Daddy Holmes's hot-licks instrumental 'Chicken Rock' and Charlie Daniels's sci-fi dance tune 'Robot Romp', but such songs had far less impact on the tastes of teenagers than the nationwide pop hits.

Despite living in this pop-dominated milieu, young people still wanted to dance to the sound of rock 'n' roll. Originating in the African American rhythm and blues sound, rock 'n' roll retained the twelve-bar blues structure and the i-iv-v chord progression of R&B, but simplified the beat, accenting the second and fourth beats of each measure. The resulting 'pa-boom, pa-boom' pattern of beats drove listeners wild and made them want to move their bodies in time to the rhythm.[1] Early observers of the rock 'n' roll phenomenon singled out the beat as the ingredient that made this new form of music so popular. For instance, in a 1964 article titled 'What Do They Get from Rock 'n' Roll?' Jeremy Larner contends that the teenager's 'need for rock 'n' roll . . . [is] a need fulfilled only by the one standard ingredient of all rock 'n' roll: its steady, heavy, simple beat'.[2] Larner goes on to say that this beat creates a 'hypnotic monotony' that causes the dancer to enter 'a kind of mystic ecstasy'.[3] In this ecstatic state, 'dream and dreamer merge, object and feeling gel: the whole universe is compressed into the medium of the beat, where all things unite and pound forward, rhythmic, regular, not to be denied.'[4] Even if Larner overstates here the possibility of entering a transcendent state of mind by feeling the beat of rock 'n' roll, no one can deny that young people responded viscerally to the music. Simon Frith explains that black music (and, by extension, rock 'n' roll) 'expresses the body, hence sexuality, with a directly physical beat and an intense, emotional sound – the sound and beat are *felt* rather than interpreted via a set of conventions'.[5] In other words, teens could enjoy rock 'n' roll emotionally and physically without having to comprehend it on a cerebral level.

Teenagers naturally wanted to feel the pleasurable sensations they derived from rock 'n' roll again and again; accordingly, dancing was the number-one social activity for teenage girls, who danced together at one another's homes or with boys at organized dances.[6] While music could be provided by transistor radios, record players or jukeboxes, no device could match the sound of a live band, with its greater amplitude and physical presence. In response to this demand for live rock 'n' roll music, at least in part, garage bands similar to The Wailers sprang up across the country. Most of them came and went without leaving much of a trace, serving as 'living jukeboxes' (to use Charlie Gillett's term) before splitting up and re-forming in new combos.[7] However, many local amateur musicians also played to express their creative impulses. They wrote and recorded their own songs, developing regional followings for their bands and helping rock music to evolve, and these are the bands we talk about today. Not surprisingly, the majority of these bands came out of regional garage-rock scenes, the most visible ones being in the Pacific Northwest, the Upper Midwest and Southern California.

Clearly defined scenes emerged in these regions because of certain conditions, the main one being the existence of a metropolitan area with a large teenage population and an active teen dance scene. In addition, the teens there had to be hungry for rock 'n' roll – usually because of a strong R&B tradition in the area – and yet have limited access to professional performers and stars, typically because the region was so far away from the major entertainment centres that professionals had only a small presence there. Teenagers on the East Coast, for instance, had less need for homegrown bands because the area was already full of professional musicians who could provide dance music. In the South, a racist and moralistic backlash against rock 'n' roll had occurred, even though the music had originated there, and white teenagers probably hesitated to dance in public to a kind of music that was so closely associated with black people. Likewise, many amateur musicians who followed in the footsteps of Elvis, Jerry Lee Lewis and Carl Perkins probably opted to play country music to avoid being stigmatized as lovers of black music; even rockabilly was considered by most Southerners to be tainted by its affinity with black music. That being said, a small garage scene with its epicentre in Memphis did emerge in the South, with the bands mainly playing R&B for fraternity and sorority dances at colleges throughout the southeastern states.[8] By contrast, garage bands in the Northwest, Midwest and Southern California embraced rock 'n' roll and played it with an almost religious fervour, developing their own regional sounds and releasing records on regional labels, many of which enjoyed local success and a few of which trickled into the national consciousness.

The Pacific Northwest

The roots of the Northwest garage sound can be traced to the number of African Americans who had migrated to the Seattle area during the Second World War to work in the shipyards, taking their musical tastes with them. In the pre-rock 'n' roll years, local hepcats were listening to R&B instrumentals such as Bill Doggett's 'Honky Tonk' and Jimmy Forrest's 'Night Train' – tunes with simple blues-based rhythm parts and elaborate melodies played on multiple saxophones and/or the organ.[9] This sound was the basis for the 'Sea-Port Beat' as laid down by Seattle's own Dave Lewis, pianist and leader of an R&B band.[10] During the rock 'n' roll years, the Dave Lewis Combo opened regional shows for Bill Haley and His Comets and were even billed as 'The Northwest's Greatest Rock 'n' roll Band' in spite of the fact that they played R&B.[11] Nonetheless, as the area's leading teen dance combo, they held sway over the first generation of rock bands formed by white teenagers, including The Regents, The Dynamics, The Viceroys, The Frantics and The Wailers, who absorbed the musical style of the Dave Lewis Combo while thinking of them as a model to follow.[12] At the same time, these fledgling bands were caught up in the instrumental rock trend of the late 1950s, so they tended to play hybrid instrumentals that combined

R&B with rock 'n' roll (except for The Wailers, who at this stage cultivated more of a true rock 'n' roll sound).

Of these bands, The Frantics stand out because they, like The Wailers, had several hits in the Billboard charts. The band formed in 1955 when guitarist Ron Peterson and accordionist Chuck Schoning started playing together in the seventh grade. After they added a drummer, bassist and sax player to the ensemble, The Frantics began performing at teen dances; before long, they were opening shows for national touring acts throughout the Pacific Northwest.[13] The band signed a recording contract with Seattle-based Dolton Records and their first hit was a tune called 'Straight Flush', which entered the charts in 1959 at about the same time as The Wailers' 'Tall Cool One'. Later that year, The Frantics' 'Fog Cutter' made it to the lowest ranks of the Billboard Top 100. Both songs typify the hybrid sound of the band, with catchy saxophone solos being played over lively, sprightly rhythms. The Frantics' tunes rely on a clean jazz-guitar sound and hummable sax melodies, creating a sound that is lighter and cleaner than that of The Wailers, whose songs rely on a bottom-heavy, dirty-toned rhythm guitar, along with honking, rhythmic sax riffs. In short, The Wailers rock harder but The Frantics have a more eclectic, fluid R&B sound. While their greatest commercial moment came when they served as Bobby Darin's backing group for his No. 2 hit 'Dream Lover',[14] The Frantics' finest artistic moment came when they recorded 'Werewolf', an offbeat soundscape that opens with a bit of dialogue from Lon Chaney Jr's film *The Wolf Man* (1941), stating that even a church-going, kind-hearted man may turn into a werewolf when the wolf bane blooms. The music consists of a steady tom-tom beat, a trebly, bubbling arpeggio and a guitar figure that sounds like the build-up to another part of a song but repeats itself over and again. Layered over that is a blend of guitar cries and cymbal crescendos as well as wolf snarls, growls and howls. 'Werewolf' made it to No. 83 in the Billboard charts in 1960, and in the late

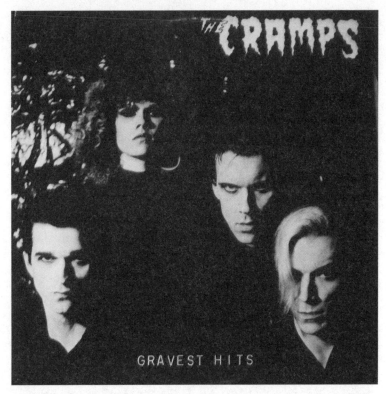

A '70s garage band, The Cramps played plenty of adaptations or covers of older songs. On *Gravest Hits* (1979), their first EP, they blended horror-movie imagery with rock 'n' roll and rockabilly covers.

1970s The Cramps found it exotic enough to rip off for their own 'Don't Eat Stuff off the Sidewalk'.

Both The Frantics and The Wailers had a huge influence on the next generation of Seattle-area bands, most notably The Sonics, who took the Northwest garage sound to its most primitive extreme. The band started off in the usual manner, with a budding guitarist named Larry Parypa being joined by a couple of friends from junior high school on drums and stand-up bass. The trio played their first gig, a birthday party, in 1960. After adding a second guitarist to the group in 1961, they began playing standards such as 'Raunchy' and 'Rumble' as well as tunes by The Ventures and The Wailers.[15] At that stage, Parypa's idols included The Wailers, whose songs he copied while learning how to play the guitar, and The Frantics, whom he respected as the area's best musicians. His combo's main goal was to sound as much like The Wailers as possible.[16] They named themselves The Sonics after the sonic booms that emanated from the nearby Air Force base; never has a more fitting name been chosen for a rock band. Parypa's older brother Andy then joined the group on electric bass, and they added a sax player and vocalist to the fold so that they could perform songs such as 'Lucille', 'Ooh Poo Pah Doo', and 'Louie Louie'. Soon, The Sonics were playing at private parties, school dances and the local teen club in Tacoma. In 1962 the band began adding more R&B-oriented material by Freddy King, Bill Doggett, King Curtis and James Brown to their sets (probably in reaction to The Wailers' own move towards R&B), and by late 1963 they were one of Tacoma's hottest teen bands.[17]

However, The Sonics lacked their own identity and sound until some personnel changes early in 1964 brought in Jerry Roslie on keyboards/vocals, Bob Bennett on drums and Rob Lind on sax. These new members roughened The Sonics' sound considerably. Roslie had a raspy, guttural voice, and although he patterned himself after Little Richard, he punctuated songs with hackle-raising screams instead of falsetto whoops, and where Little Richard was flamboyant and exuberant, Roslie was macho and menacing. Bennett was a powerhouse drummer who walloped the hell out of his kick drum and made his snare beats crack like rifle shots. The other members bought larger Fender amps and turned up the volume to the point of distortion. According to Larry Parypa, it was the new combination of personalities that made them more aggressive; they gave up trying to play like The Wailers or The Frantics and began 'assaulting' their material.[18] When Buck Ormsby, part-owner of Etiquette Records, auditioned the boys for a record deal, he yawned through their Wailers covers but wanted to jump for joy when they pounded out their first original, 'The Witch', a song about the dangers of trying to make a move on a strange, black-haired girl who enjoys tormenting men. Impressed by The Sonics' loud, dirty sound and Roslie's screaming, Ormsby signed them to Etiquette, and 'The Witch' was released as a single in November of 1964, becoming a regional hit that sold over 25,000 copies.[19]

By then, The Beatles had taken over the country, but they had no real influence on the sound of The Sonics, who responded to Beatlemania mainly by wanting to grow their hair longer.[20] Kids loved the raucous, hard-hitting music of The Sonics; in the words of Roslie, 'people liked it because we'd lay it down real hard. The beat was just BOOM! BOOM! . . . It was good for dancing.'[21] Success came quickly and easily and The Sonics played as far afield as Pittsburgh and Cleveland, but because they could make $1,000 a night playing in Seattle, they turned down gigs in such places as San Francisco and Northern California.[22] Their complacency and teenage irresponsibility also caused them to quit rehearsing and to play only at gigs, spending the rest of their time partying.[23]

Eventually, self-doubt crept into their minds as they compared themselves to more proficient bands. Larry Parypa recalls, 'Our feeling was we weren't legitimate because we couldn't play rock 'n' roll with great finesse and understanding of the music. When we would play with some local band that maybe had horns and were good musicians, Gerry [sic] and I always felt like maybe we shouldn't be there.'[24] In other words, the band members wondered if their abrasive, all-out approach to playing rock 'n' roll was a gimmick or a novelty rather than real musicianship. Still, they managed to record their debut album, *Here Are The Sonics*, by early 1965, and it shows that they were way ahead of their time. Roslie wrote lyrics about girls, cars and obsessive relationships just like other teenage songwriters, but his take on these things was dark and twisted. The original gems on this album include 'Psycho', 'Boss Hoss', 'He's Waitin'', 'Shot Down', 'The Hustler' and 'Cinderella', but the best is probably 'Strychnine', a song about the pleasures of getting high on rat poison. Another hard-pounding rocker, 'Strychnine' has a minor-scale chord progression that gives it a sinister tonality. It has proven to be a garage classic, having been covered by many other bands, such as The Cramps, and gives credence to the notion that The Sonics invented punk rock before anyone knew what to call it.[25] Even if this claim does overlook the contributions of Link Wray and a number of rockabilly songs, no one can deny that The Sonics had a proto-punk sound and attitude. No music critic ever told them that they were doing anything worthwhile back in their day, and yet they went on to release an even rawer album called *Boom* (1966) while wondering if their primal approach to rock 'n' roll was legitimate or not.

A scene parallel to the one in Seattle developed about 175 miles to the south in Portland, Oregon, spawning two of the most commercially successful garage bands in America: The Kingsmen and Paul Revere and the Raiders. The saga of The Kingsmen and 'Louie Louie' began in 1959 when two childhood friends named Jack Ely and Lynn Easton began playing together. With Ely on guitar and vocals and Easton on drums, the two played a long-term gig at a yacht club and then added Mike Mitchell on lead guitar and Bob Nordby on stand-up bass to become a real rock 'n' roll combo.[26] In 1960 the band took on the name The Kingsmen, which Easton's mother registered at the courthouse. Ken Chase, the programme director at KISN Radio, then hired them to be the house band at his teen nightclub.[27] The band first witnessed the power of 'Louie Louie' when they were resting between sets at the Pypo Club in 1961 and noticed that the kids were playing The Wailers' version over and over on the jukebox and dancing to it.[28] They learned the song and played it at their gigs after that, even going so far as to play it repeatedly for ninety minutes straight at a show in April 1963.[29] The next day, Chase took them into a studio to record their infamous version of the song. Calling it a wrap after the boys had recorded one warm-up take, Chase had Jerden Records of Seattle press up

1,000 copies of the single, of which the band managed to sell about six hundred copies.[30]

Meanwhile, Easton staged a hostile takeover of the band, announcing that henceforth he would be the frontman and play the saxophone while Ely would be moved back to the drums. The others laughed at the absurdity of such a change, but Easton reminded them that his mother owned the rights to their name and that he could do whatever he wanted with the band. Ely and Nordby left in a huff.[31] Then, in October of 1963, after some deal-making and fortuitous events, 'Louie Louie' broke out in Boston and the single was picked up by the Wand label of New York.[32] The single kept selling, peaking at No. 2 in the Billboard charts the following January, right before The Beatles took over with 'I Want to Hold Your Hand'.[33] To make the most of this turn of events, Easton hired a new drummer and bassist and began touring to support the hit record. Ely responded by touring with his own new band, Jack Ely and the Kingsmen, an action that caused recriminations and lawsuits to fly back and forth.[34] Once a settlement had been reached, Easton and his version of The Kingsmen profited the most, living on in several incarnations as America's premier frat/party band and succeeding way beyond their level of talent; not only did 'Louie Louie' sell over 7 million copies, but the band sold 20 million records in all, placing eight singles and five albums in the Billboard Top 100.[35]

Paul Revere and the Raiders, The Kingsmen's competitors and music-scene buddies, rose to even greater heights. The Raiders got their start in Caldwell, Idaho, where a piano-playing youngster named Paul Revere Dick began pounding the keys for an R&B group led by vocalist Red Hughes. Revere was also a teenage entrepreneur; after leaving high school, he became a barber and owned three barber shops by the age of eighteen. He sold those and bought the Reed and Bell burger stand, which he used as a platform from which to promote the teen dances he organized.[36] One day, while picking up burger buns at the local bakery, Revere ran into an aspiring rock 'n'

After the phenomenal success of 'Louie Louie', The Kingsmen became America's premier frat-rock combo.

roller named Mark Lindsay. The teenager sang for a rockabilly band called the Idaho Playboys, but he soon began sitting in with the Red Hughes band. Not only did Lindsay play sax, he also had good looks, stage presence and a great voice, so eventually the band dumped Red Hughes and adopted Lindsay as their frontman.[37] Taking the name The Downbeats, the band played covers of The Wailers songs as well as their own piano-driven instrumentals. Revere took a demo tape of their tunes down to Los Angeles to shop around, luckily crossing paths with John Guss, who owned a record-pressing plant and ran a small label named Gardena Records.[38] Guss loved Revere's material but had the band change their name to Paul Revere and the Raiders before releasing eight 45 rpm singles for them between 1960 and '63.[39] The first single, 'Beatnik Sticks', was a boogie-woogie take on 'Chopsticks' that became a hit on the West Coast from Los Angeles to Vancouver,[40] and the last was a remake of The Wailers' 'Tall Cool One' single. In between, the third single was 'Like, Long Hair', a boogie-woogie spoof of Rachmaninoff's Prelude in C# minor. This one rose to No. 38 in the Billboard charts by April 1961, and Dick Clark was about to have the Raiders appear on *American Bandstand* when Revere got his draft notice. While he was able to declare Conscientious Objector status because of his Mennonite background, he was nonetheless sent to serve in a psychiatric facility outside Portland, Oregon, thus ending this part of his ride.[41]

The next leg of the Raiders' career involved a rivalry with The Kingsmen and duelling versions of 'Louie Louie'. After Revere's release from service in the summer of 1962, he and Lindsay met up in Portland and reformed the band. They hired local musicians, two of whom were part-owners of a teen club called The Headless Horseman; in short order, the Raiders became the club's house band.[42] After being exposed to 'Louie Louie' and having the usual conversion experience, the Raiders began playing the song at their shows. They also took on a new manager, Roger Hart, who was a popular DJ and dance promoter. Before long, Hart noticed the effect that 'Louie Louie' had on dancing teenagers and took the guys into Northwestern, Inc. in April 1963 to record it – in the same week that The Kingsmen recorded it at the same studio.[43] Hart put the record out on his own Sande label, and the two recordings of 'Louie Louie' began duelling for airplay on the local radio stations.[44] Then Hart got the Raiders signed to Columbia Records in June 1963, which was a coup of sorts, but Columbia was not a rock label and lacked the savvy to push the record.[45] By contrast, The Kingsmen's 'Louie'

With humble beginnings in Caldwell, Idaho, Paul Revere and the Raiders went on to become the most commercially successful garage band of the 1960s.

was on Wand, a black R&B label in New York that buried the Raiders' 45 nationally by pushing their own record vigorously on radio stations in the East.[46] It should also be admitted that The Kingsmen's 'Louie' was much more exciting than the Raiders' more competent but uptight take on the song.

The Kingsmen may have won the battle of the Louies, but the Raiders won the war of commercial and artistic success. Although The Kingsmen sold plenty of records, they were never more than a glorified bar band, whereas Paul Revere and the Raiders became one of the greatest American rock bands of the mid-to late 1960s. The British Invasion transformed them from a New Orleans-style rock 'n' roll band into an AM radio juggernaut that took on elements of the new British style but retained the power of their Pacific Northwest roots. Indeed, their publicist Derek Taylor, who was also the original press agent for The Beatles, promoted them as 'the American answer to the British Invasion'.[47] However, it was the Raiders' music that sold records; in hits such as 'Just Like Me', 'Hungry' and 'Kicks', they displayed a heavy but melodic sound, with hard-stomping beats, monster riffs and low-pitched harmony vocals that tickled the listener's insides. Their infectious sound, coupled with plenty of television exposure, made them the most successful garage band of the 1960s, demonstrating that the pop music industry of that time was still open to fresh and innovative sounds no matter where they came from – even the garages of the Pacific Northwest.

Southern California

Further down the Pacific coast in the Los Angeles area, local bands concocted a mutant strain of instrumental rock called surf music, but it took some time for this style to evolve. In the beginning, young people were dancing at beach parties to the same records that kids in the Northwest were dancing to – instrumental tunes such as Bill Doggett's 'Honky Tonk', The Ventures' 'Walk Don't Run' and Freddy

King's 'Hideaway'. They were also fond of The Virtues' 'Guitar Shuffle Boogie', The Duals' 'Stick Shift', Lonnie Mack's cover of 'Memphis' and drummer Sandy Nelson's LPs *Teen Beat* and *Let There Be Drums*.[48] In 1959, the beach-romance movie *Gidget* popularized the bohemian surf lifestyle and suddenly thousands of teenagers in the area took up surfing. Several do-it-yourself film-makers such as Bud Browne and Bruce Brown began filming surfers in action and splicing the footage together to create documentaries. They toured from town to town and showed their films in schools and civic centres; for soundtracks, they would play reel-to-reel tapes of Hawaiian music, flamenco guitar music and rock instrumentals by Duane Eddy, Link Wray, Johnny and the Hurricanes, The Fireballs and The Wailers.[49] Thus teenagers began to associate these kinds of music with surfing.

In the meantime, young Californian guitarists were listening to the guitar parts in tunes such as The Ventures' 'Walk Don't Run' and The Fireballs' 'Bulldog' and getting ideas about the sounds they wanted to create.[50] 'Bulldog' was recorded in Clovis, New Mexico, and The Fireballs' lead guitarist, George Tomsco, played his twangy licks on a Fender Jazzmaster through an echo chamber to convey a sense of the wide-open spaces of the desert Southwest.[51] According to Kent Crowley, author of *Surf Beat: Rock 'n' Roll's Forgotten Revolution* (2011) Tomsco's guitar sound appealed to Californian musicians because they were living between the vast expanse of the Pacific Ocean and the open terrain of the interior West, and the spacious sound seemed to suggest the possibility of adventure and limitless opportunity out there in the wide-open world.[52] The first few records by local musicians to reflect these influences as well as the SoCal beach-going lifestyle included The Gamblers' 'Moon Dawg!', The Revels' 'Church Key' and The Frogmen's 'Underwater', all of which may be called 'proto-surf' records.[53] The next phase of proto-surf music occurred on two different fronts; in the South Bay area, a garage band named The Belairs began hosting dances at

Hermosa Beach and Redondo Beach that were well-attended by local surfers, and the innovative guitar playing of Paul Johnson and Eddie Bertrand began to be copied locally.[54] In 1961 The Belairs scored a regional hit with their atmospheric 'Mr Moto'.[55] Meanwhile, on Balboa Peninsula off Newport Beach, Dick Dale and His Del-Tones were packing in the teens at the Rendezvous Ballroom; they played there for three years and pulled in as many as 4,000 kids per night. Dale had an aggressive double-picking style of playing his Fender Stratocaster, putting out a roaring sound in his attempt to express the power of the ocean waters as well as the feeling of riding the waves on a surfboard.[56] The surfing crowd loved the power of Dale's playing and did the 'Surfer's Stomp' to his music.[57] Like The Belairs, Dick Dale had his first regional hit in 1961, with 'Let's Go Trippin',[58] and dozens of garage surf bands started up in his wake, imitating his playing style as well as his compositions.

One quality that sets genuine surf music apart from plain instrumental rock is the use of sound-modifying devices to simulate the experience of being in the marine environment. The most important of these effects is reverberation, and, as was noted earlier, several of The Wailers' tunes would be called surf music if the guitar parts only had more reverb on them. Reverberation occurs when a sound in an enclosed space echoes back to the listener from different angles and distances while decaying back to silence. When used on a guitar signal, reverb makes the notes take on a 'wet, splashy' sound and can give the listener a sense of watery open space, as if the notes are being bounced around under a pier or a covered marina.[59] Following the example of Dick Dale, surf guitarists learned to mute the strings with their right hand and use hard, staccato picking to make explosive plunking sounds when they played the notes of a melody. The stand-alone reverb unit that Fender Electric Instrument Co. first made available in 1961 also made other watery noises; containing a reverb spring inside an oil-filled tank, it would not only make dripping, popping and sizzling sounds on its own, but it would also make the sound of a crashing wave when it was bumped or jarred. Surfers in the audience associated these noises with what they heard inside waves, making them relate to surf music even more.[60]

Another important effect came from the vibrato tailpiece, which allowed a guitarist to bend the pitch of a note up or down by pushing down or pulling up on a 'whammy bar'. By wiggling the vibrato arm up and down, a guitarist could create a striking 'wow-wow-wow-wow' sound that suggests undulating waves. In the hands of a skilled user, it could also be used to imitate the sound of a lap-steel guitar or Hawaiian guitar, thereby evoking those kinds of music.[61] More significantly, the instability of pitch caused by using a vibrato bar suggests groundlessness, a lack of firm support under one's feet while trying to stand on a floating platform, such as the deck of a boat or a surfboard, which can lead to a feeling of vertigo and even cause the listener to feel queasy or seasick. Moreover, surf guitarists learned how to pluck the strings while holding the whammy bar in their right hand so that they could end a lick or a chord with a downward pitch bend and cause the sound to die away in the way that a wave dies out; conversely, they could bend the pitch up to suggest the swelling of a wave before it crests. These movements added emotional colour to the guitar sound, expressing either decay or growth, which in turn could suggest death or hope and optimism. Thus a guitarist could create tension or resolution as he played, altering the mood of the song as it progressed. Typically, surf tunes alternate between dark, gritty passages and bright, hopeful ones, causing the listener to feel either tension or optimism. Some songs that have these qualities include The Belairs' 'Mr Moto', The Vistas' 'Moon Relay' (which is full of downward pitch bends on the lead guitar riffs) and 'Batman' by The 4 of Us, which uses pitch bends in addition to a descending minor-key riff to give the listener a sense of freefalling.

These selections illustrate another quality that separates surf from normal instrumental rock, and that is harmonic content. To be sure, many great surf tunes are nothing more than rip-roaring rock 'n' roll tricked up with reverb. 'Woody Wagon' by Manuel and the Renegades, a Latino surf combo, rocks and rolls with a dirty-toned guitar and raunchy sax solo. Other examples include The Vulcaines' 'Cozimotto', The Reveliers' 'Hanging Five' and The Mockers' 'Madalena'. In The Ree-Gents' 'Downshiftin' one can hear whammied, 'downshifted' chords in the I-IV-V chord progression. All these tunes are fun to listen to, but more harmonically adventurous surf music gets away from this progression and the dominant seventh chords of rock 'n' roll. For instance, many surf tunes hark back to the music of surfing documentary soundtracks by using chord changes borrowed from flamenco music. The scale used in flamenco moves one half-step up (or one fret up on a guitar) from the first note to the second, which gives this scale its exotic flavour. Surf music that contains flamenco-type chord progressions or riffs sounds moodier and less 'plain vanilla' than straight rock 'n' roll – The Surf Teens' 'Moment of Truth', The Road Runners' 'Quasimoto' and The Fender IV's 'Everybody Up', for example, all employ the flamenco cliché of playing a barre chord on one fret and sliding up to the next fret to play that chord before moving back to the first chord.

Another way that surf bands twisted the harmonic content of rock 'n' roll was by adding minor chords and riffs in minor keys to their compositions. This practice began with The Belairs and 'Mr Moto', which not only avoids the twelve-bar blues structure but starts with a catchy riff played in D minor.[62] Usually, people feel that the minor scale has a gloomy or ominous quality, but The Belairs' lead guitarist plays the signature riff with a snappy, up-tempo feel so that it takes on an air of intrigue or mystery, sounding more like the theme from a spy movie than a dirge. Many a teen surf band followed suit, sometimes even using minor-key riffs in songs that are otherwise structured as rock 'n' roll; Five More's 'Avalanche' is a good example of this approach. Others use the alternating structure described above, so that the tension created in one section by tough, menacing lower-register riffs is relieved by a passage of brighter, more harmonious, trebly riffs. Zorba and the Greeks' 'Shockwave' and Mickey Aversa's 'Blast Off' both use this approach, and the minor-key riffs in the lighter parts sound wistful rather than sombre, as if the musicians are trying to express some yearning for adventure or fulfilment of some kind.

The other leader in expanding the sonic palette of surf was Dick Dale (born Richard Anthony Monsour), whose Lebanese heritage caused him to bring Middle Eastern melodies to surf music. Dale's earliest musical influence was an uncle who taught him how to play the darbuka, a goblet drum. The rapid, pulsating beats he played on that instrument showed up later in his life as the rapid-fire double-picking he does on his Stratocaster. As a boy, Dale also watched his uncle play the oud, a lute-like instrument used in much Middle Eastern music, at the annual Lebanese festival in Boston, while other relatives belly-danced.[63] These early influences surfaced in Dale's surf remake of 'Misirlou', a traditional song from the Eastern Mediterranean region that originated in Egypt or Asia Minor and which exists in Greek, Jewish, Armenian and Turkish versions.[64] The scale it uses is very similar to the Phrygian mode used in flamenco music, but it sounds very different from flamenco-style surf music; even with Dale's fast-tempo, reverb-laden treatment, the song sounds like ethnic folk music.[65] Local surf-music fans loved it, and the tune reached No. 1 on the Hollywood radio station KFWB in 1962.[66] Teen surf musicians also loved Dale's new, exotic sound, covering 'Misirlou' more than any surf tune other than The Surfaris' 'Wipe Out'. Dale followed it up by writing a couple more instrumentals that sounded like Middle Eastern folk songs, 'The Victor' and 'The Wedge', spawning a host of stereotypical imitations such as The Jesters' 'A-rab', The Silvertones' 'Bathsheba', Dave and the Customs' 'Ali Baba' and Jim Head and His Del Rays' 'Harem Bells'.

The highly imitative nature of teen garage bands underscores the fact that musicians who played instrumental rock were constantly searching for the million-dollar sound or riff that would send their records to the top. Lacking lyrics and the vocal performance of a well-known personality, instrumental rock depended upon novel sounds. Accordingly, several trends came and went during the surf movement; one subgenre was hot-rod music, which capitalized on the SoCal obsession with customizing cars and building hot rods. It was basically surf music mixed with the roar of drag racing, usually in stereophonic sound so that the thunderous roar will pass from left to right. Always quick to jump on a trend, Dick Dale released several albums' worth of hot-rod music, including *Checkered Flag* (Capitol 2002), *Big Hot Rod Hits* (Capitol 2024), and *Dick Dale, Bo Troy and His Hot Rods* (Diplomat 2304).[67] A subgenre of hot-rod music was motorcycle music, the lyrics of which focused on motorbikes rather than customized cars, with groups such as The Hondells recording songs such as 'Little Honda', 'Hon-Da Beach Party', 'Black Boots and Bikes' and 'Haulin' Honda'.[68] Another surf-music trend reflected the contemporary interest in space-age technology and outer space, with titles such as The Phantoms' 'x-L3' and The Vistas' 'Moon Relay'. Other tunes, such as The Centuries' 'Outer Limits' and The Starfires' 'Space Needle', mixed 'outer space' sounds or the sounds of rockets and satellite telemetry with the musical content of surf songs.

The hunger of garage musicians for new material, coupled with their tendency to gravitate towards cool new sounds, explains why bands around the country jumped so quickly on the woody wagon of surf music when it left the confines of Southern California. In 1963, The Surfaris' 'Wipe Out', The Chantays' 'Pipeline' and The Pyramids' 'Penetration' all received national airplay and entered the upper reaches of the Billboard pop charts along with surf pop songs by The Beach Boys and Jan and Dean. Vocal surf pop was far more popular with the teenage listening audience, but garage musicians would have been unable to mimic the vocal harmonies of The Beach Boys and their ilk, and besides, they were more attracted to the radical guitar sound of instrumental surf music. Before long, teen guitarists all over America were shredding their picks like Dick Dale and writing outstanding surf instrumentals that can compete with anything from Southern California: bands such as The Clashmen of Tucson, Arizona; The Astronauts of Boulder, Colorado; The Trashmen of Minneapolis, Minnesota; The Centuries of Hazlet, New Jersey; The Creations of Milford, Connecticut; and The Vistas of Rochester, New York, among others.

The genre became so popular among American garage bands that some of them continued to write and record surf instros well into

Most surfing movies from the 1960s included performances by one or two surf combos. In this still shot from *Surf Party* (1963), The Astronauts give the partygoers a heavy dose of reverberating Fender sound.

1966, long after Beatlemania made the surf movement irrelevant. The larger significance of the surf idiom is that it became part of the general language of rock music. The use of reverb, vibrato bars, minor-key riffs, exotic musical scales and so on became absorbed into the rock guitarist's arsenal, and surf-style riffs began showing up in mainstream rock songs, including The Beatles' 'I Feel Fine', The Rolling Stones' 'Satisfaction' and The Monkees' 'I'm a Believer'.[69] Such examples reveal just how important teen garage bands have been in causing rock music to grow and evolve.

The Upper Midwest

The Upper Midwest, a huge region comprising North and South Dakota, Minnesota, Wisconsin and Michigan, was another hotbed of garage rock during the pre-Beatles years. The musical epicentre for this region was Minneapolis, Minnesota, the northernmost major city on the Mississippi River. Not only did Minneapolis have a healthy population of youngsters who were hungry for entertainment and wanted to bop to the Big Beat of rock 'n' roll, the city had the infrastructure to support a musical scene, boasting plenty of radio stations, record stores and venues for teen dances. It also had a record-production facility in Kay Bank Recording Co., which could master and press records in addition to recording music on tape, so all the local record labels such as Soma, Bangar and Garrett used them for manufacturing records.[70] Local musicians sprouted up in this nurturing environment; inspired more by country and western, rockabilly and classic rock 'n' roll than by the R&B of their counterparts in the Pacific Northwest, these musicians began playing orthodox rock 'n' roll for their audiences in the late 1950s.

One of the earliest and most influential garage bands in Minneapolis was Mike Waggoner and the Bops. One day in 1957, when Waggoner was sixteen and working at his uncle's gas station, Gene

Vincent pulled up to have his big Lincoln serviced. A star-struck Waggoner decided to get into the rock 'n' roll game himself, recruiting his brother Colly to play lead guitar, Sheldon Hasse to play bass and John Lentz to play drums. Their musical influences included Gene Vincent himself as well as Conway Twitty, Jerry Lee Lewis and The Everly Brothers, and the Bops started playing rock 'n' roll for teen dances at the Crystal Coliseum, a Quonset hut out in the suburbs. After becoming regulars on the regional touring circuit, they recorded a single at Kay Bank Studios; it has Dale Hawkins' 'Baby Baby' on the A-side and a rockin' instrumental called 'Basher No. 5' on the B-side. Released on the local Vee Records, the single racked up some airplay in the Twin Cities and the Bops became local legends who inspired many other combos to start up.[71]

One such combo was The Trashmen, the biggest name among garage bands of the Midwest. Founding members Tony Andreason (lead guitar), Dal Winslow (rhythm guitar) and Steve Wahrer (drums and vocals) all got their start by playing in various local combos, the most notable one being Jim Thaxter and the Travelers, who, according to Mike Waggoner, had a 'basic Carl Perkins-type sound'.[72] After the Travelers released a single featuring 'Sally Jo' and 'Cylcon' in 1960, the group left Jim Thaxter, and Andreason went into the army. The three former bandmates got back together and reformed as The Trashmen in 1962, naming themselves after a song called 'Trashman's Blues' by local trash-rock eccentric Kai Ray.[73] With Bob Reed on bass and drummer Wahrer singing most of their material, the band played obscure rock 'n' roll songs by Jerry Lee Lewis and Buddy Holly in addition to oddities such as Warren Smith's 'Ubangi Stomp' and Paul Chaplain and his Emeralds' 'Nicotine'.[74] Late in 1962, Andreason, Winslow and Wahrer went out to California for a vacation and stayed on Balboa Beach, where they were able to see surf acts such as The Chantays and Dick Dale and His Del-Tones perform. Impressed by Dale's pick-shredding, the band went back home to Minneapolis and began playing surf tunes such as 'Misirlou' and

'Hava Nagila' in addition to the usual instrumentals by The Ventures and Link Wray. They also started performing their other material, such as Chuck Berry songs, surf-style, and local teens went crazy for it. As guitarist Winslow explains, 'the kids in Minneapolis were ready for it.'[75] Area musicians were ready for this new sound too, adopting it and spreading the movement in the Upper Midwest.

In fact, a band from Duluth, Minnesota, named The Titans were already playing surf-style music with vocals when The Trashmen discovered it. Working as Dale Allen and the Rebel Rousers, they released a single called 'Hideaway' in 1962;[76] musically, 'Hideaway' is a slow-tempo, melancholy song with some reverb-laden surf riffs, but it also has a vocalist singing lyrics that tell some girl to go back to where she came from and hide herself! As it turns out, many surf songs in the Midwest follow the same pattern, laying vocals over an instrumental-style track that sounds nothing like the bouncy and upbeat surf pop of The Beach Boys. Another example in the same vein is the haunting 'High Himalayas' by The Yetti-Men of Minnetonka, Minnesota, recorded in the spring of 1964 and released on an LP that featured The Yetti-Men on one side and The Uppa Trio on the other.[77] Even The Trashmen have vocals on their first surf recordings from 1963, 'Surfin' Bird' and 'King of the Surf'; however, they would go on to record cover versions of classic surf instrumentals such as 'Baja' and 'Malaguena', just as The Titans would release three more conventional surf instros in 1963 and '64, and The Yetti-Men would record surf instros 'Blue Surfer' and 'Break Time' in 1964.[78] Other notable surf tunes from the region include '80 Foot Wave' by The Vaqueros of Virginia, Minnesota, 'Riptide' by Impact v of Minneapolis and 'Take 7' by The Novas of Edina, Minnesota, a group that also had a nationwide hit in 1964 with a Trashmen-inspired novelty song called 'The Crusher', their tribute to a Minneapolis wrestling legend named Reginald Lisowski (aka The Crusher).[79]

Another surf tune that obviously parodies The Trashmen's 'Surfin' Bird' is The Jades' 'Surfin' Crow', a novelty instro that adds the cawing of a crow to a track similar to 'Malaguena'. The Jades' drummer explains that the song was named 'Surfin' Crow' in order 'to take a swipe at surfin' music',[80] but it seems likely that The Jades were also taking a jab at The Trashmen – not that anyone took offence at the parody. Guitarist Andreason even bought a copy of 'Surfin' Crow' and showed it to people because he found it amusing.[81] The Trashmen could afford to be magnanimous because 'Surfin' Bird' was their ticket to international renown. The song rose to No. 4 in the Billboard charts early in 1964, and Andreason believes that it would have gone to No. 1 if not for some stiff competition from a ditty called 'I Want to Hold Your Hand'.[82]

When 'Surfin' Bird' hit No. 4, Dick Clark wanted the band to be on *American Bandstand* in Los Angeles, but the show would only pay airfare for one member, so Wahrer flew over and did the bird dance in front of an audience as the song played – something he found to be somewhat humiliating.[83] The band was also slightly embarrassed by the legal hassle that loomed when The Rivingtons sued The Trashmen's record company for copyright infringement; after all, 'Surfin' Bird' is a mash-up of the black R&B band's hits 'Papa-Oom-Mow-Mow' and 'The Bird's the Word' – but The Trashmen had only heard a band from Milwaukee play the songs when they began to improvise 'Surfin' Bird'. The affair was settled when their record company agreed to give The Rivingtons credit for writing 'Surfin' Bird'. After that, the band composed 'Bird Dance Beat' and 'Bird '65' in the same vein, and no one made a peep.[84] The Trashmen would go on doing the bird dance beat until they lost their sense of direction and called it quits at the dawning of the Summer of Love, but their body of work has made them one of the combos most revered by garage-rock aficionados. That said, The Trashmen were not the only band in town; according to one estimate, there were about four hundred bands in the Twin Cities by 1964, and The Accents, The Underbeats and Gregory Dee and the Avanties were considered by locals to be the best.[85]

Similar bands emerged in neighbouring Wisconsin, where the biggest scene was found in Milwaukee. In 1963, radio station WRIT sponsored a city-wide battle of the bands, and about fifty local combos entered.[86] One of the most prominent bands in the early days was formed by Sam McCue, a working-class youth from the south side. Attracted to the electric guitar after seeing the hot

Promo photo of The Trashmen, Minnesota's premier surf band and one of America's greatest rock 'n' roll bands before the Beatles Invasion.

guitarist in a Latin big band, McCue began playing one himself.[87] He also listened to western swing, Louis Jordan's R&B, rockabilly, blues and rock 'n' roll, and by 1958 he had put together The Nomads, a rock 'n' roll band that would evolve into The Legends and play the circuit of teen dances and beer bars.[88] The Legends released six or seven singles before the Beatles Invasion, the most notable ones being 'Lariat', an instrumental from 1961, and 'Bop-A-Lena', an echo-drenched cover of Ronnie Self's rockabilly raver from 1962.[89] About 75 miles to the northwest, another scene developed in the Fox River Valley, where the minimum drinking age was eighteen, as opposed to 21, and the beer bars attracted plenty of youngsters looking for a good time.[90] One of the most successful groups to come out of this setting was The Catalinas, a rock 'n' roll band that played one-nighters throughout Wisconsin before becoming the house band at The Quarry, a beer bar in Appleton. The group also released three 45s before the Beatles Invasion, the best one being 'War Party' in 1962. In autumn 1964 The Catalinas became the second white group to be signed by Chess Records, for whom they recorded an LP, but the label balked at the idea of releasing a rock record. To set themselves apart from the other combos out there on the lounge circuit, The Catalinas changed their name to The Golden Catalinas and adopted an all-gold look, bleaching their hair and wearing sparkly gold clothes and boots. The golden boys remained a popular attraction into the late 1960s, playing as far afield as Utah and Pennsylvania and releasing several more singles after the British Invasion.[91]

The same pattern can be seen across the border in Michigan, where an early garage band named The Galaxies formed in Iron-wood. Playing in the style of Buddy Holly, Eddie Cochran and Gene Vincent, The Galaxies were performing at teen dances in upper Michigan and northern Minnesota by 1959. In September that year, the band went to Kay Bank Studios and recorded 'If You Want to Be My Baby', a vocal number, and 'Ad Lib', an instrumental rocker.[92] Vocalist Dan Sullivan had a good voice for singing in the manner of

Elvis and Ricky Nelson; on the strength of his vocals and the band's guitar riffing, The Galaxies were signed to Guaranteed Records of New York, who put out their next single, 'My Tattle Tale (I'm Gonna Tell My Mommy on You)'.[93] The 45 was promoted heavily from Detroit to Milwaukee, where it hit No. 40 in the local charts, and The Galaxies performed throughout the region, but it all came tumbling down when two of the members got married in late 1961, a typical end for a garage band.[94] Over on the far eastern border of Michigan in Detroit, rough-and-ready instrumental rock boomed alongside the Motown sound. One of the prime movers in this scene was Lenny and the Thundertones, formed in 1959 by Lenny Drake (lead guitar), Peter Weiss (rhythm guitar) and Al Johnson (bass). In 1960 and '61, not long after the owner of a record store across the street from their high school became their manager, the Thundertones cut two singles for Dot; 'Hot Ice' is a crude rocker with out-of-tune Chuck Berry-type licks, backed by distorted power chords played à la Link Wray. 'Thunder Express', the group's signature tune and third single, was released in 1961. This raw, guitar-based instrumental has a main riff with plenty of Duane Eddy-style twang as well as a drum solo in the middle. All told, Lenny and his boys ended up releasing six thunderous 45s before the Beatles Invasion. A similar group was The Thunder Rocks, whose primitive novelty song 'What's the Word' features a shouted question-and-answer vocal refrain and a sax solo. Other bands working in the same vein include Johnny and the Hurricanes, The Royaltones, The Teen Beats, Aladdin and the Genies and The Sunliners, all of whom helped to set the stage for the Motor City hard-rock sound that would emerge later.[95]

As one can see, teenagers were bopping to the rhythms of home-grown rock 'n' roll all over America before The Beatles came along and changed the course of American popular music for good. In terms of national chart action, the last hurrah of unadulterated American garage rock can be heard in The Trashmen's 'Surfin' Bird' and The Rivieras' 'California Sun'. 'Surfin' Bird' entered the Billboard

Top 100 charts on 25 January 1964, staying in the charts for thirteen weeks and peaking at No. 4. Then 'I Want to Hold Your Hand' appeared, entering the charts on 1 February and spending fifteen weeks in the charts, seven of those at No. 1. Next, The Rivieras, a frat-rock/garage band from South Bend, Indiana, hit with 'California Sun', a surf-rock song with a catchy guitar part that celebrates the good life on the California beaches. 'California Sun' entered the Billboard charts on 29 February 1964, spending ten weeks in the charts and peaking at No. 5.[96] It goes without saying that 'Surfin' Bird' and 'California Sun' both would have reached No. 1 or 2 had they not been kept down by The Beatles' hit. For a while, American garage bands had a tough time making any sort of a nationwide splash until the media feeding frenzy that accompanied The Beatles' arrival in America jump-started a second wave of garage rock in the mid-1960s.

2

The Creators:
The Garage-Rock Supernova
in Mid-1960s America

One of the most electrifying moments in American pop culture was made possible by television. Just as appearing on television shows had helped to catapult Elvis Presley to national celebrity, such exposure propelled The Beatles to international stardom and fuelled Beatlemania.[1] This process began in the UK, where millions of viewers not only watched the lads from Liverpool perform on shows such as *Thank Your Lucky Stars* and *Sunday Night at the London Palladium,* but witnessed thousands of frenzied London youths scrabbling and jostling to get a clear look at their idols.[2] American television viewers began seeing the same footage in November 1963, when the Huntley-Brinkley Report on NBC News ran a story on Beatlemania that showed just how crazed The Beatles' fans could be. Jack Parr ran similar footage on his show for 3 January 1964, providing some mocking commentary for the benefit of his adult audience.[3] In the meantime, Capitol Records spent $50,000 on a marketing campaign designed to pull American teenagers into the Beatles craze before the Fab Four arrived for their first visit to the States.[4] The ploy worked; when the band touched down at the airport in New York City, thousands of screaming pubescent girls, along with a crowd of amazed onlookers, were on hand to greet them. Hundreds of besotted girls assaulted the group's limousine and later tried to break into their rooms at the Plaza Hotel.[5] This scene was duplicated in Washington, DC, and

Miami; elsewhere in America, people had to experience the bedlam vicariously by watching news reports. The most pivotal broadcast, of course, occurred on 9 February on *The Ed Sullivan Show*, which featured The Beatles performing a few of their hit songs live. Viewers watched as over seven hundred girls in the studio audience danced and clapped, laughed and cried, shook their locks, put their hands over their faces, fainted and screamed as the foursome played and sang. More than 60 per cent of the American television audience – some 73 million people – watched this media event.[6]

After seeing the effect that The Beatles had on girls, many a pubescent boy decided that he wanted to get in on the action, including Phil Bleecker of Memphis, Tennessee, who went on to become a vocalist for The Poor Little Rich Kids.[7] Paul Teitelbaum, a member of The Blue Chips from Rego Park, New York, states: 'The day after The Beatles' appearance, [it] was all over. Every kid I knew ran out and bought a guitar.'[8] Similarly, Chris Curtis of The Sonics writes, 'From the first glimpse of Ringo on the Ed Sullivan show, I knew more than anything in the world, I wanted to play the drums. It was my destiny.'[9] Perhaps the most eloquent description of this desire comes from Craig Moore of Iowa's GONN, who writes,

It was great to be a teenager in 1964, to witness the debut of The Beatles on American TV, and be old enough to actually fantasize about reaching that *outrageous* pinnacle – to be on TV, to make your own records – to have all those wild, beautiful girls going berserk every time you open your mouth, shake your head, to have 'em scream bloody murder just at the mention of your name! Whew, looked like a mighty good job to me![10]

Like most teenagers, Moore failed to see the downside of being chased by mobs of half-crazed girls who would tear their idols' clothes to pieces in order to have some kind of contact with the objects of their desire. Other would-be musicians were encouraged by the apparent simplicity of The Beatles' music and stage act. For example, Wayne Wadhams of Stamford, Connecticut's The D-Men writes, 'I was inspired by The Beatles like everyone else. I remember seeing them on the Ed Sullivan show and thinking, "Neat tunes. Simple. I can do that".'[11] A similar statement comes from Mark Volman of the pop group The Turtles, who writes, 'when The Beatles came along, we all stopped and looked at what we were doing and said, "Hey, we could actually do this!"'[12] In his case, he was in a band that 'made it', unlike the vast majority of teenage musicians, who thought the path to stardom would be smooth and easy because of the apparent quickness of The Beatles' rise to the top.

In addition, more perceptive youngsters noticed that adults were obsessed with The Beatles; no matter how much grown-ups made fun of the pop stars' haircuts and musical abilities, they were fascinated by the Fab Four. At press conferences, news reporters and public officials asked the bandmates all kinds of inane questions, which they fielded with witty, irreverent and playful aplomb, making their questioners look like dull-witted clods and the mop-tops appear to be in control. The sight of a bunch of shaggy-haired musicians being taken seriously by clueless adults impressed youngsters no end, and they wanted to be in the same position. Accordingly, the number of garage bands in America exploded after the Beatles Invasion. Evidence of this can be seen in various cities; Milwaukee, for example, had about fifty combos in 1963 and over two hundred by 1966 or '67.[13] Likewise, only a handful of rock 'n' roll bands existed in Memphis before 1964, but four or five hundred of them sprouted up during the mid- to late '60s.[14]

As already noted, this growth resulted in a huge increase in sales of electric guitars, drums and harmonicas.[15] A large portion of the beginners who bought these instruments probably formed groups with like-minded peers once they had learned to play a few rudimentary songs, and, although it might be an exaggeration to say that every single town in America harboured at least one active combo, it would be safe to say that every community was within 20 or 30 miles of a town that did.

At this stage, two kinds of garage bands emerged, one made up of beginners and the other made up of experienced musicians in pre-existing bands; these latter sensed that a paradigm shift was imminent and adapted to the new British style as quickly as possible.[16] In an attempt to recreate some of that Beatles magic, both kinds of garage musician imitated the Fab Four's style, growing their hair longer and wearing skinny ties, jackets with narrow lapels, stovepipe pants and Spanish flamenco boots. The Guilloteens of Memphis, for instance, changed their look to fit the new pattern and chose their name because they thought it sounded English.[17] More established bands did the same thing and also imitated The Beatles' sound. The first group to do so and have a national hit was The Chartbusters, a 1950s rock 'n' roll band formerly known as Bobby Poe and the Poe Kats. After moving from Kansas to Washington, DC, in the early 1960s, The Chartbusters cut a song called 'She's the One' in response to the Beatles Invasion and it 'busted' into the charts in 1964.[18] Another band from the DC scene was The British Walkers, who originally called themselves Bobby Howard and the Hi-Boys and whose members included well-known blues guitarist Roy Buchanan. Their debut single, 'I Found You', is a Liverpudlian pop ballad with a Bo Diddley beat and wailing harmonica.[19] Further south, The American Beetles became Miami's answer to the Fab Four after beginning their existence as a 1950s rock 'n' roll band called The Ardells and changing their name in 1964. They released five Beatlesque singles that same year, but none of them resulted in American Beetlemania.[20]

The quintessential Beatles sound-alike hit is The Knickerbockers' 'Lies', which made it to No. 20 in the pop charts in 1965. The Knickerbockers formed in New Jersey and were already a well-known club act in New York when the Invasion took place.

After being signed to Challenge Records and moving to Los Angeles, they recorded the song that displays many stylistic traits of the Beatles' sound and idealizes them in one powerful pop composition. First off, the main riff in 'Lies' is adapted from the opening chords of 'I Want to Hold Your Hand', and the lead vocalist sings in a John Lennon-like strained, raspy rock 'n' roll voice. The song also features a McCartney-style scream during the break as well as Ringo-style drum rolls and fills.[21] The chorus includes cheery melodies and sweet harmony vocals, and each chorus part builds to a catchy, climactic refrain sung in a falsetto voice. The song is anchored by bubbling, bobbing bass runs and the guitar parts are played aggressively with a grainy, distorted tone. However, it would be a mistake to write 'Lies' off as mere mimicry, for it is a clever, well-conceived pop song in its own right.

One of the reasons that The Beatles' music seemed so fresh and exciting to American listeners is that it was only partially based on rock 'n' roll; it also drew upon R&B, soul, country and doo-wop. The Beatles were, in fact, working in the genre known as 'beat music', a form that had been developed by British groups in the nightclubs of Hamburg, Germany.[22] The rhythmic intensity of beat music – whence comes the name – had its origins in the rhythms of skiffle, a musical form that was born in the rent parties held by African Americans in New Orleans during the 1920s and '30s.[23] The repertoire of skiffle included American folk music of the kind played by Lead Belly and Woodie Guthrie, songs such as 'Rock Island Line', 'John Henry' and 'Cumberland Gap'. Lonnie Donegan, the leading figure of skiffle, played these songs in the genre's fast-tempo style with a dance-band rhythm section – consisting of rhythm guitar, stand-up acoustic bass and full drum kit.[24] Local amateur skifflers in Britain followed suit, even when their rhythm sections had to use makeshift instruments such as drums fashioned from pots and pans and basses made out of broom handles and tea chests.[25] The homegrown skifflers who stayed in music ended up in beat bands and took the rhythms of skiffle with them to Hamburg, where they were also exposed to the *mach schau* (literally meaning 'Make show!' but roughly meaning 'Let's go!') beat, used to encourage audience participation by having people clap and stomp along with a 4/4 beat.[26] The insistent pounding four times per measure made this rhythm different from the rhythm of rock 'n' roll, which puts a strong emphasis on every second and fourth beat of a measure. Thus beat musicians in Hamburg took the principle of the *mach schau* beat and turned it into a flexible stomp beat that could be used to give 'rhythmic propulsion' or a 'simple dance beat' to any kind of music, no matter how unrelated to rock 'n' roll it might be.[27]

Apart from rhythm, beat music derives its song structures, harmonic content and melodies from all kinds of popular music, not just rock 'n' roll. In the case of The Beatles, their music was most influenced by Chuck Berry, Buddy Holly and the Crickets and Carl Perkins, while their vocal style was distilled from the singing of Little Richard, The Shirelles, The Drifters and The Miracles. With great facility, The Beatles digested these raw materials and worked them into highly original and inventive songs that appealed to a very large audience.

The stupendous success of The Beatles opened the American market to other British beat groups, most notably Gerry and the Pacemakers, The Searchers, The Animals and The Dave Clark Five. For a time in the mid-1960s, The DC5 even sold more records in the United States than The Beatles. The music of these groups came to be known as Merseybeat or the Mersey Sound because they hailed from Liverpool, through which flows the River Mersey. Because of Merseybeat's domination of radio playlists in America in 1964 and '65, garage musicians began to turn their attention to pop music. Suddenly, instrumentals were out and vocal pop music was in. A massive wave of garage pop appeared, with the melodic hooks, vocal harmonies and infectious rhythms expected of pop, but the rough-hewn production values and primal nature of garage pop kept it from being as cutesy and sappy as regular pop. An ideal example may be heard in Half Pint and the Fifths' cover of 'Loving on Borrowed Time', a northern soul-style song recorded by Phil Orsi and the Little Kings of Chicago.[28] Orsi's song about the wrongness of continuing an illicit love affair contains some deliciously dissonant chord changes and a verse that turns dark and foreboding, but the lyrics are sung in harmonized vocals, the backing track mainly consists of horn parts and the slick production gives it a splashy 'showbiz' feel. The Fifths, a garage band from Chicago, transform 'Loving' into a rock song by playing the horn parts on a guitar and giving it more rhythmic punch with a full drum set and a tambourine. The drummer also makes great use of drum rolls to punctuate and build up tension in certain parts of the chorus. Moreover, Half Pint sings the verses solo in his nasal, garage-punk voice and uses minimal vocal harmonies in the chorus. In their hands, the song loses its glitz and gains power, with the dissonant bits and the strong melodies standing out even more.

To be sure, garage pop runs the gamut from hard-rocking power pop to soft and syrupy bubblegum pop. An example of the hard approach may be found in 1967's 'I've Gotta Way with Girls' by The Lavender Hour, a band from Houston, Texas.[29] A ballsy guitar part dominates the music, with the main riff consisting of a Chuck Berry-style, double-stopped, string-bending lick that moves down the neck of the guitar. Balanced against the forceful guitar playing is the pleasing harmony of the main vocal, sung in unison by several British-sounding male voices. The chorus part seems especially geared towards AM radio, with a thick and punchy mass of voices singing a sugary melody. A similar song from 1967 is 'Don't Mess Around with My Dream' by The Penthouse Five from Dallas, Texas.[30] The body of the song features loud, deep bass lines and highly rhythmic strumming on the guitar, along with some power chords; over that, the melody is sung by a smooth male voice with plenty of tremolo, and the back-up vocals are sung in high-pitched harmony. Again, what we hear in garage pop of this kind is the combination of opposing elements, with harmonized pop-style vocals being set against forceful, aggressive instrumental parts. A more well-integrated song is 'Liar, Liar' by The Castaways, who were formed at the University of Minnesota in 1962.[31] The main riff is played on a creepy-sounding organ; at the end of each organ riff, we hear a high, keening guitar lick, and each verse begins with two lines sung in a falsetto voice. The break in the middle of the song begins with a short bass solo and a scream before going into a crude guitar solo. The resulting concoction is incredibly catchy; 'Liar, Liar' rose to No. 12 in the Top 100 during the summer of 1965, and it has come to be considered a garage classic.

Other garage pop takes a more stereotypical approach to achieving the pop sound, with songs that are designed to appeal to the sentimental moods of teenagers. A good example is 'I Wonder' by The Gants, a band from Greenwood, Mississippi, that supported The Animals on one of their early tours of the States.[32] The Gants had a considerable songwriter in vocalist/guitarist Sid Herring, and his skills are on display in 'I Wonder', a song about a young man who wonders why he feels so funny inside and shy around the girl of his affections. The song's main riff, played on the low strings of the guitar and descending down the neck, is melancholy and bittersweet, and Herring's almost girlish voice quavers with tremolo. The backing vocals consist of simple ooohs and aaahs, and one can picture teenage girls sighing wistfully while listening to the voices in 'I Wonder'. Another song using the feminized voices of pop music is The Gestures' 'Run, Run, Run', which tells a girl that she needs to run away and be free after cheating on her boyfriend. The Gestures were a major band in the 1960s Minneapolis scene, and 'Run, Run, Run' made it to No. 44 in the Billboard charts in 1964.[33] In keeping with the times, the guitars and drums play a driving British-beat rhythm, and the vocals carry the melodies. Sung in unison by a couple of singers, the vocals are so lush and mellifluous that one could easily get the impression that women are singing instead of young men, and combined with the catchy phrasing of the words and the effective use of stops and starts to build tension, the vocals make 'Run, Run, Run' a very pleasing song. Other garage-pop songs use choirboy vocals to hook the listener, as in 'They Don't Know' by The Trolls of Chicago.[34] Here, a throbbing bass part propels the song, and a slightly fuzzy guitar motif is repeated at key moments. The lead vocalist sings in a clear, boyish voice, while the backing singers echo words from the lyrics in addition to singing nonsense syllables such as 'doo-doo-doo-doot', 'ooo-ooo-ooo-ooo', and 'aah-aah-aah-aah', resulting in pretty, melodious sounds that appealed to many teenage girls. These examples are a mere drop in the ocean of garage pop, but they are typical enough to show that British beat music had a softening effect on American garage music, causing it to move away from conventionally male-oriented subjects like surfing and hot rodding towards subjects such as lamenting lost love or finding romance.

British-style R&B

The second major branch of American garage rock engendered by the British Invasion was British rhythm and blues, a style rooted in the British blues movement. Of course, long before the Brits had much exposure to blues or R&B, a number of white musicians and enthusiasts in America sought out and listened to the music of African American artists. Recall that members of The Wailers frequented the Evergreen Ballroom near Tacoma to see artists such as Little Richard, Ray Charles, Bobby 'Blue' Bland and Junior Parker perform.[35] When The Beatles were serving their rock 'n' roll apprenticeship in Hamburg, The Wailers had already created a full-blown R&B revue, adding songs by Ike and Tina Turner, Etta James and bluesman Freddy King to their repertoire.[36] At the same time over in England, members of the nascent Rolling Stones were listening to records by black R&B and blues artists. Keith Richards was turned on to the blues by hearing Big Bill Broonzy first and then Robert Johnson and other Delta bluesmen; Brian Jones had near-religious experiences after hearing Elmore James and seeing Muddy Waters perform in concert; and Mick Jagger was crazy about the recordings of Chuck Berry, Bo Diddley, Muddy Waters and Little Walter.[37] Not surprisingly, after The Rolling Stones formed and became the house band at the Crawdaddy Club in London in February 1963, they were playing raw covers of songs by many of their idols.[38] Eventually, because the British Invasion gave them so much influence in the United States, bands such as The Rolling Stones and The Yardbirds popularized blues among American teenagers and kicked off a new genre of garage rock.

In the beginning, The Rolling Stones took pride in being true to the African American music they performed. As Keith Richards explains, they were blues 'disciples' who wanted nothing more than to help sell records for Jimmy Reed, Muddy Waters and John Lee Hooker.[39] Yet they inevitably altered the music they tried to recreate for consumption in London nightclubs, speeding up the tempos and changing the rhythms of the originals. Michael Hicks notes that when the Stones recorded Waters' 'I Just Want to Make Love to You', they made the tempo twice as fast as the original.[40] The Yardbirds, who succeeded The Rolling Stones as the resident band at the Crawdaddy Club, likewise sped up the tempos of their R&B covers; for example, Bo Diddley's 'I'm a Man' has 80 to 85 beats per minute (bpm) and Muddy Waters' version has 70 to 75 bpm, but The Yardbirds' version has 140 to 145 bpm. Hicks reasons that Bo Diddley and Waters express their strength and virility through a slow, pounding beat, emphasizing force and mass, whereas The Yardbirds assert their manliness through 'youthful energy', emphasizing action instead of force.[41]

British R&B bands also modified the beats of the blues songs they covered in order to intensify the rhythms. For instance, the Stones were fond of using the 'rhythmic monad' of beat music, putting an accent on every beat of a measure to create a regular and unsyncopated series of strong pulses, the persistence of which suggests 'pure power'.[42] In songs of their own such as '(I Can't Get No) Satisfaction' and 'Paint it Black', the Stones introduced the rhythmic monad beat to a worldwide audience. The Yardbirds also modified the beats of the R&B songs they covered, being especially fond of pseudo-double time, a technique that makes a song sound as if it is moving twice as fast as it actually is. In pseudo-double time, the drummer shifts from using a backbeat (with the second and fourth beats accented) to an offbeat ('1 and 2 and 3 and 4 and', with the second part of each beat being accented).[43] The Yardbirds used this technique to invent the rave-up, a passage in which the players build a crescendo by playing in pseudo-double time more and more intensely until they reach a dynamic climax.[44] Usually, the drummer would pound on his ride cymbal to build up a wave of noise while the bassist and guitarists would apply rapid up-and-down strokes to their strings, simultaneously running their fingers up the neck so that the notes became higher and higher in pitch and more raucous. At the end of the rave-up, the band would return to the normal beat, which would make for a stunning break in the song, or the band would abruptly end the song with bravura. Either way, the effect had a dramatic impact upon audiences, as one can hear by listening to The Yardbirds' live versions of 'I'm a Man' or 'Smokestack Lightning'.

Needless to say, American garage musicians took to this new sound right away and began imitating the techniques used by British R&B bands to intensify rhythm. One of the most well-known examples of the rave-up being used in American garage music is Count Five's 'Psychotic Reaction', a two-part song with a lyrical section and a freak-out section that creates a musical analogy for the singer's 'psychotic reaction'. The song opens with a cranky fuzz-guitar riff and some harmonica warbling; then the drummer plays a monadic beat and the rhythm guitarist strums back and forth on two chords, giving the lyrical section a bouncy feel, while the vocalist sings a verse about being starved for love and affection from a girl who has lost interest in him. At the end of the verse, the band launches into the 'psychotic reaction', a double-time rave-up that features a fuzz guitar freak-out, a pulsating bass line and some reverb-laced 'chukka-chukkas' from the rhythm guitar. This chaotic and tension-filled part ascends in pitch until the climax is reached, and then the song goes right back to the snappy, upbeat section, where we hear the second verse, and then it ends with the same rave-up, copied directly from The Yardbirds' cover of 'I'm a Man'.[45] Rip-off or not, 'Psychotic Reaction' tickled the ears of the record-buying public enough to become a No. 5 hit in the pop charts during the summer of 1966.

Other garage musicians became interested in their own cultural heritage because of British R&B and began covering African American blues songs in the British manner. A good example is the D.C. Drifters' raucous version of Muddy Waters' 'Louisiana Blues', a song played by Waters with a lazy tempo and very spare instrumentation. Waters uses a slide guitar to play the main blues riff, a harmonica to play the melody and two sticks to tap out the rhythm. The D.C. Drifters turn 'Louisiana Blues' into a British-style R&B song by increasing the tempo, giving it a rock 'n' roll drumbeat and, using an organ and a reverb-soaked guitar instead of slide guitar and harmonica, playing Waters' slide riff as the motif of the song. The break features a wildly distorted guitar solo, and the song ends with a guitar freak-out in addition to the band members laughing and whooping it up before the fade.

To see just how much rougher American garage bands could get than their British mentors, it is revealing to contrast The Rolling Stones' cover of Slim Harpo's 'I'm a King Bee' with that of The Bad Seeds from Corpus Christi, Texas. Harpo's original is an understated blues shuffle with the vocals way up front in the mix, and the drumbeat is a simple backbeat with the hi-hat playing eighth notes. In the final measure of each movement there is a swooping sound made on the E string of a guitar; every now and then, we hear a high 'stinging' note to suggest a bee sting. The Rolling Stones play their version pretty much the same way, except that the drumbeat is much more emphatic and relentless, and they play the swooping sound and the stinging sound more regularly. Mick Jagger even enunciates like Harpo when he sings. By contrast, The Bad Seeds dispense with the swooping sounds and intensify the rhythm by making the rhythm guitar much louder in the mix, with the guitarist playing his chords in a jangly, bouncy way. The lead guitarist's tone is raunchy and loaded with reverb, and he hits the strings hard to get a strained, buzzing sound; when he plays his solo, he goes a little crazy in bending the high strings to get some stinging notes. On top of that, singer Mike Taylor's voice has some Texas twang in it, not the drawl of an African American bluesman. The boisterous, unrestrained sound of covers like these indicates that American garage bands were much less concerned than the Stones about being true to the blues.

Of all the African American R&B and blues artists, the one most revered and imitated by rock groups was Bo Diddley, who gave the world his 'Bo Diddley beat', a rhythm sounded out by the following words: 'shave and a haircut – two bits'. Many 1960s bands used this beat in their own compositions (The Strangeloves' 'I Want Candy', for example), or they covered Bo's songs because they were attracted to his highly rhythmical and eccentric sound, which was due in part to Bo's primitive guitar style but also to the maraca player he always had to shake some more rhythmic action into his songs. British groups such as The Rolling Stones and The Pretty Things mimicked him, developing what George R. White calls the 'long hair and maracas' school of British R&B.[46] American garage bands followed the lead of their British models, covering such Bo Diddley classics as 'Road Runner', 'I'm a Man', 'Bo Diddley', 'Mona (I Need You Baby)' and 'Who Do You Love?' in the style of British R&B but making their versions a little rougher and more abrasive. A well-known cover of 'Who Do You Love?' was released by The Preachers, a garage-punk band from Los Angeles, in 1965. The Preachers give the song a hard-driving, relentless backbeat, and vocalist Richard Fortunato sings the lyrics in a tough, grainy voice, but what makes their recording so notorious is their throat-ripping delivery of the chorus part, with three different voices coming in one at a time, 'aah – aah – aah', each one screaming in harmony at different pitches. Another rough-and-ready cover is the Homesick Blues' take on 'Mona'. This band from New Jersey gives the song a loud, thumping 'Bo Diddley' beat, shaking maracas on every beat. The drummer also throws in some tribal-esque tom-tom fills, and the guitarist uses Bo's descending guitar warble to good effect, double-picking the strings and running his fretting hand down the neck of the instrument. To get that authentic wobbly, shimmery sound that Bo used, the guitarist also uses a big dose of tremolo and reverb. These two examples are only the tip of the iceberg; in *Bo Diddley: Living Legend*, George R. White lists 42 covers by American garage bands, and 24 garage songs, that mimic Bo's style.[47] Bo Diddley may have been disappointed by the number of records that he sold

The Whisky a Go Go was the leading club on the Sunset Strip in Los Angeles and it hosted many a show by area garage bands during the 1960s.

during his career, but his music lived on and reached a widespread audience through the efforts of his garage-band disciples.

Folk Rock

The third major branch of garage music is folk rock, which essentially involves playing folk songs with electric guitars and full drum kits. Typically, folk songs have a message or express some social commentary and are performed by the songwriter, accompanying themselves on an acoustic guitar. These traits show up in folk rock, the beginnings of which can be heard in the vocal harmonies and jangly twelve-string guitar strumming of The Searchers, the Merseybeat group that covered songs like 'Needles and Pins' in this style.[48] However, the most important and influential purveyors of the folk-rock sound were The Byrds, a group that had a symbiotic relationship with Bob Dylan and which was founded on the idea of melding Dylanesque folk with The Beatles' vocal harmonies.[49] Their recording of 'Mr Tambourine Man', with its bright, chiming guitar sound, delicate harmonies, soul-stirring melodies and thought-provoking words, became a No. 1 hit and made The Byrds into America's answer to The Beatles.[50] Their success also sent Dylan's career into overdrive; by the end of 1965, folk rockers had covered 48 of Dylan's songs, with many of them becoming hits, including The Turtles' 'It Ain't Me Babe' and Cher's 'All I Really Want to Do'.[51] In the summer of 1965, Dylan himself scored a No. 2 hit with 'Like a Rollin' Stone'.[52] This barrage of hits made folk rock the 'it' sound of the year and ushered in a 'new lyrical consciousness' that caused songwriters to begin writing meaningful words in the manner of Dylan.[53]

One of the most overlooked and underappreciated groups in this movement is The Beau Brummels, who were the first rock band of any note in San Francisco and the first to play in the style of folk rock,[54] although their sound owed more to The Everly Brothers than to Dylan. They were also one of the few groups in San Francisco that wrote their own material, most of it by guitarist Ron Elliott, who enjoyed using minor keys because they added an air of mystery to the songs. The band's other significant weapon was their vocalist, Sal Valentino, who had a strong, resonant voice with a wide pitch range. These strengths can be heard in their first hit, 'Laugh, Laugh', which balances a melancholy Merseybeat sound on the verses against an uplifting pop chorus. The song shifts smoothly from major to minor chords and displays rich vocal harmonies as well as the trembling but powerful voice of Valentino and the lonesome wail of a harmonica. 'Laugh, Laugh' made it to No. 15 in the charts in 1964, but their second single did even better, rising to No. 8 and beating 'Mr Tambourine Man' to the charts by a month.[55] 'Just a Little' sounds more folky than the first single, mixing plangent single-note riffs on an acoustic guitar with the trebly, shuddering chords of an electric guitar. The verse has ascending minor-key harmony vocals behind the shimmering vocals of Valentino, and the chorus shifts into a soaring, higher-register blast of harmonized vocals.[56] The Beau Brummels would release two albums in 1965 and place seven songs in the Billboard Top 100, but their hits reached ever lower levels in the charts. With their small record label lacking promotional muscle, and the band always seeming to be out of step with the times, The Beau Brummels never lived up to their commercial promise.[57]

Another accomplished garage band that had trouble finding widespread success was The Bluethings (or The Blue Things) of Hays, Kansas. Starting off in 1964 as The Blue Boys, the group played Merseybeat-inspired folk rock and became incredibly popular in the Midwest as a live act.[58] The creative force in the band was Val Stecklein, a folk singer and songwriter who was energized by the music of the British Invasion and Bob Dylan. Some of The Bluethings' songs obviously emulate Dylan's music, as in 'Waiting for Changes', a solemn number played on the acoustic guitar and sung by Stecklein with the phrasing and articulation of Dylan. 'Girl of the North

Country' is even more reminiscent of Dylan; played by the full band with drums, bass, harmonica and acoustic and electric guitars, the rousing, country-flavoured song has Stecklein half-speaking, half-singing the words in a husky, Dylan-like voice. Other songs such as 'You Can't Say We Never Tried' and 'Pennies' sound more like The Searchers: an acoustic guitar plays rhythm, electric guitars play tremulous Merseybeat riffs, a tambourine's jangle augments the rhythm here and there and a harmonica plays lonely melodies. Moreover, Stecklein's vocals have an appealing sonority, with the backing singers providing rich, transparent harmonies. On the strength of their first couple of singles, RCA signed The Bluethings in 1965 and released an album called *The Blue Things* in 1966. Though now considered a minor classic in folk rock, the LP sold poorly, not helped by the radio programmers who found the lyrics of 'Doll House', a song about the victimization of prostitutes in brothels, to be offensive.[59] Meanwhile, the band heard The Beatles' *Revolver* and became caught up in psychedelia, covering several Beatles' songs while putting on legendary live shows. They went on to record three psychedelic singles in September 1966, the best one being 'The Orange Rooftop of Your Mind', but by May 1967 Stecklein had left the group to pursue a solo career and The Bluethings faded away, unable to build up much of a following outside Texas, Oklahoma and Kansas.[60]

The majority of garage bands lacked the artistic gifts of The Bluethings or The Beau Brummels, but they could imitate the jangly guitar sound of The Byrds. Mike Markesich refers to this strain of teenage folk rock as 'jangle-beat' and explains that the bulk of these songs lack lyrical sophistication and focus on the favourite subject of teenage boys: girls.[61] Such songs are generally built around a trebly riff or arpeggio, usually played on the high strings of a twelve-string guitar, and the moods of the songs range from introspective and downcast to inspiring and upbeat.[62] To be sure, garage bands did play other forms of folk rock unrelated to jangle-beat. After The Animals

During the heyday of teen rock 'n' roll combos, producers of low-budget movies in Hollywood began including garage bands in their films to appeal to the younger set. In this shot from *The Cool Ones* (1967), The Leaves are seen playing their song 'Dr Stone' in a fictitious nightclub on the Sunset Strip.

scored a smash hit in 1965 with their adaptation of 'House of the Rising Sun', a traditional American folk song recorded previously by Woodie Guthrie and Lead Belly, every guitarist in the country had to learn the sad, stirring arpeggios of The Animals' version, and every teen combo had to cover the song. Another huge hit among garage bands was 'Hey Joe', a song with murky origins in the folk scene of Greenwich Village.[63] After The Leaves had a Top 40 hit with their folk-punk recording of 'Hey Joe' in the spring of 1966, it became one of the most covered songs of the mid- to late '60s, turning into another 'Louie Louie'. More significantly, the popularity of folk rock helped garage bands to get beyond the dominant seventh chords and twelve-bar blues structure of rock 'n' roll, just as surf music had done earlier. In this way, garage bands were being prepared for the coming of psychedelic music and its harmonic innovations.

Sixties Garage Punk

Another sonic revolution took place during the folk-rock boom, one that was triggered in May 1965 by The Rolling Stones' hit '(I Can't Get No) Satisfaction'. Keith Richards' use of a fuzz box to get that bold, angry tone on the song's main riff suddenly made fuzztone *the* effect for guitars, and it quickly showed up in all kinds of music, from recordings by garage bands to themes for popular television shows such as the American sitcom *Green Acres*.[64] A distorted guitar sound was nothing new, of course. In the early 1950s, many rhythm-and-blues guitarists turned up the volume on their small amplifiers, overdriving the tubes and overloading the speakers, to get a raunchy timbre like that of a saxophone,[65] a practice that The Wailers followed later to get the dirty guitar tone on their instrumentals. As previously mentioned, Link Wray in 1958 poked holes in the speaker of his amplifier before recording 'Rumble' to roughen up the timbre of his guitar, and Larry Parypa of The Sonics did the same thing with an icepick in the early 1960s.[66] Most musicians of the mid-'60s, however, found it more convenient to plug their guitars into a fuzz box, a device that clips off the peaks of the sound's waveforms and causes distortion. Using fuzz, a guitarist could give his or her instrument 'its own peculiar vocal "grain" or sonority', a recognizable voice with more character than a clean guitar. This voice was often angry and hostile, and fuzztone became a tool for 'masculine' expression, with the male youth of the period participating in a new 'machismo aesthetic' by making aggressive, hormonally 'overdriven' musical statements about their status in a society in which they were subordinate to adults.[67]

The use of fuzztone to express adolescent frustration and aggression later came to be associated with the idea of 'punk', a term that has a long and convoluted history in the discourse of rock music. Legend has it that Ed Sanders of The Fugs coined the term 'punk rock' in 1970 while describing the music on his *Sanders' Truckstop* album for an interviewer.[68] A year or two later, when record collectors and fanzine writers began looking back with fondness at '60s garage rock, they used the 'punk' label in reference to the immaturity of the musicians. For instance, in the autumn 1971 issue of *Who Put the Bomp*, Greg Shaw defines punk rock as 'white hard rock music made by teenaged bands during the mid '60s',[69] the operative word here being 'teenaged'. Lenny Kaye, the man who compiled the first-ever collection of 1960s garage music in 1972, describes punk rock in the album's liner notes as music played by 'young' and 'decidedly unprofessional' teen groups that 'exemplified the berserk pleasure that comes with being on-stage outrageous, the relentless middle-finger drive and determination offered only by rock and roll at its finest'.[70] Here, Kaye focuses on the attitudes of these juvenile rockers, suggesting that their 'punk-ness' comes from a snotty, defiant urge to impose their 'barbaric yawps' on the rest of humanity

The Stones' smash hit with 'Satisfaction' made fuzz guitar the 'now' sound of the mid-1960s, and every electric guitarist had to go out and buy a fuzz box like the Gibson Maestro.

despite their lack of musical skill. However, Kaye's selections on *Nuggets* include many pop songs that would never be labelled as punk by most listeners, and his definition fails to discriminate among different kinds of garage music.

In the mid-1970s, Phil Hardy and Dave Laing provided a more comprehensive and descriptive definition by observing that '60s punk bands exhibit 'a stance of spoiled suburban snottiness' and that their music includes fuzztone on the guitars, an 'arrogant snarl' in the vocals, and lyrics dealing with 'uncooperative girls or bothersome parents and social restrictions'.[71] In short, 1960s punk bands tried to achieve what The Rolling Stones created in 'Satisfaction', even if the lyrics written by the average teenager fell short of Jagger's insights. Moreover, David Dalton suggests that Richard's distorted riff in 'Satisfaction' expresses 'menace, arrogance and incitement', qualities that reinforce the lyrics and Jagger's delivery of them;[72] American garage punks tried to do the same things in their songs, playing hard-edged, raucous music to express their own alienation and discontent. To complicate matters, however, the New Wave movement of the mid-1970s came along and co-opted the word 'punk', which then took on a whole new set of connotations, although one can find parallels between the attitudes of '60s punks and their '70s descendants. Today, musicologists prefer to use the term 'punk' for the musical phenomenon of the 1970s, and the term "60s punk' is considered to be obsolete.[73]

Be that as it may, the descriptive label "60s garage punk' still seems necessary for referring to a subgenre of garage music that has extremely transgressive qualities and which can take any form (except for straight pop), including rock 'n' roll, R&B, blues, frat rock, folk or psych. Most songs tend to be based on British-style R&B because it already had the toughness that American youths were looking for, but garage rockers exaggerated the harshness of British R&B to create a cruder, snottier and more abrasive sound. For example, in 'Sweet Young Thing' or 'Are You Gonna Be There (At the

Love-In)' by The Chocolate Watchband, one can hear Jaggeresque vocals and Stones-inspired R&B, 'but the songs are played with such barely repressed fury and sung with such imperious swagger that they have a tense, menacing tone one rarely hears in a Stones song'.[74] Some other, more obscure examples would include The Grim Reapers' 'Two Souls', an intense R&B song that has a pounding stomp beat and a thudding bass part that oscillates between two notes for most of the song. The singer has a Jaggeresque voice, but he plays around with the sounds of the words 'two souls' in the manner of Iggy Pop, and the lead guitarist makes springy 'boing' sounds instead of playing proper blues licks. In The Circus' 'Bad Seed (You're a Bad Seed)', the raspy-voiced vocalist sings about being a born loser who is as wild as a weed and who has been sent to Parchman Farm (the notorious prison farm in Mississippi where

In this shot from another teensploitation movie, *Riot on Sunset Strip* (1967), The Chocolate Watchband plays its ferocious brand of garage-punk R&B for the crowd in a mock-up of Pandora's Box, a famous club on the Sunset Strip.

many black convicts slaved their lives away). As he sings about escaping and getting revenge on the people who sent him there, he emits a sardonic, creepy 'fake' laugh, and elsewhere in the song he makes comments that manage to sound both goon-like and unnervingly perceptive. Thus the singer creates a disturbing persona who sounds dangerous, going way beyond the machismo of British Invasion bands.

Another characteristic that separates garage punk from ordinary garage music is its resistance to the established order and rejection of social conventions and expectations. As youth culture bloomed in mid-1960s America, young people began seeing themselves as being more 'with it' than the adults and 'squares' around them. This belief in hip superiority led to garage-punk songs about enlightenment, about knowing 'where it's at'. In The Groupies' R&B-punk masterpiece 'Primitive', vocalist Ronnie Peters tells some straight individual that he loves and lives 'primitive', and that what squares have to pay for he gets for free. A stronger statement of personal enlightenment may be heard in The Third Bardo's 'I'm Five Years Ahead of My Time', a stirring piece of psych-punk in which Jeffrey Monn explains in a raw masculine voice that he is now living in a new dimension and that society can no longer play with his mind. It is this sort of belief in hip superiority that causes Michael Hicks to argue that garage music is the avant-garde of '60s rock. He explains that the participants in an avant-garde movement see themselves as 'a chosen people' and insist on their difference from the masses, the greatness of their art and the need to express antagonism against conservatives and their values.[75] This antagonism can readily be seen when garage punks complain about being judged by squares for their unconventional appearance. In The Savages' clangorous 'The World Ain't Round, It's Square', the vocalist tells his girlfriend that straight people stare at them and laugh at them because of the length of their hair. In 'No Friend of Mine', The Sparkles' snotty vocalist makes the same complaint, telling his girlfriend about being called a clown and a loser by some man on the street who thinks that his hair is too long. Similarly, in The Illusions' 'City of People', the singer tells a girl that people out in public put him down and call him a clown because his hair is too long and his heels are too high. Garage-punk songs of this kind portray enlightened, hip youths as outsiders and victims of a conservative, judgemental society.

A different strain of garage punk expresses antagonism towards women, which Hicks suggests was derived from The Rolling Stones' attitudes in songs such as 'Satisfaction', 'Stupid Girl' and 'Under My Thumb'.[76] Indeed, a large number of garage-punk songs are about rejecting some girl because she has proven to be vain, deceitful, self-serving, unfaithful, unsupportive or otherwise flawed.[77] For example, in The Ugly Ducklings' highly rhythmical folk-punker 'She Ain't No Use to Me', the singer compares his unsatisfactory girlfriend to a series of useless things such as a door without a key and a sting without the bee, saying he is glad to see her leave. In another driving folk-punk song called 'Little Girl', which was a Top Ten hit for The Syndicate of Sound in 1965, the vocalist laughs about his girlfriend's infidelity and belief that she has kept it secret from him, but he also reveals that her transgressions have hurt him and he doesn't want her around anymore. Similar scenarios and attitudes may be found in The Basement Wall's 'Never Existed' and Bohemian Vendetta's 'Enough', among others.[78]

Such songs give the impression that teenage girls of the 1960s were 'no-good, lying bitches', to use Greg Shaw's mocking phrase;[79] just why this view was so prevalent during that time is a complex matter, but at the heart of it lies the sexual insecurities of teenage boys. These young men were probably somewhat aware of the changes being brought about by the sexual revolution and sensed that the liberation of women would make girls more available as sexual partners, but also that girls' increasing freedoms would make their affections that much less predictable. To fortify their psyches against disappointment, teenage boys adopted hard-hearted attitudes and created songs in which they had the power to reject females before being hurt themselves; therefore, we can see these songs as male fantasies that empowered young men, however unrealistically.[80] Another point to keep in mind is that these youthful songwriters borrowed stock phrases, images and scenarios from the colourful world of adult relationships as sung about in African American blues and R&B songs; as ludicrous as it may be for a white, suburban, high-school kid to sing about his baby coming back home to him or leaving him on the midnight train, the more important consideration is whether or not a garage song uses these borrowed tropes to make a compelling musical statement.

All-girl Garage Groups

Even though women in America have always performed music, and all-female bands existed before the advent of rock 'n' roll, teenage girls felt comfortable banding together in rock combos only after the British Invasion had sparked a pop-music renaissance. By then, the women's liberation movement was gathering force and social attitudes were beginning to loosen up. Young women felt freer to jump from being spectators and adoring fans to active performers and objects of admiration. Yet those who did form their own bands and perform in public had to overcome sexism and doubts about their abilities and motivations. The story of The Pleasure Seekers, the most active and accomplished all-girl group of the 1960s, illustrates the challenges facing female garage bands. Formed in Detroit, Michigan, in 1964 by Patti and Suzi Quatro, along with Nan and Mary Lou Ball and Diane Baker, The Pleasure Seekers got their start in the music business when Dave Leone let them play three songs at The Hideout, a nightclub that hosted such well-known acts as Bob Seger, Ted Nugent, ? and the Mysterians, The Rationals and MC5.[81] After the girls proved to be a draw, Leone put out their first 45 rpm record on Hideout Records, featuring 'Never Thought You'd Leave Me' and

'What a Way to Die'. When The Pleasure Seekers moved on to play venues other than The Hideout, club-goers would initially laugh at the sight of girls trying to be rockers, but their stage presence and self-assured playing would shut the sceptics up. Boys would crowd the stage in curiosity and their girlfriends would try to pull them away, while the male bands got a kick out of seeing girls play heavy rock music.[82] However, according to Patti Quatro, the real resistance came from music-industry types, who wanted them 'to go tits and ass, Vegas style'.[83] The Pleasure Seekers were seen as a novelty, and record-label execs wanted them to sound more pop, but the group had no interest in such music.[84] The band played on, graduating from the teen club and college circuit to concert halls and festivals, eventually being signed by Mercury Records and moving to New York City. By that time, they had worked up a Motown-style revue and a *Sergeant Pepper* revue in addition to playing some acid rock, but once again, executives at Mercury pressured the girls to go down the 'pop/T&A route'; Quatro adds that Mercury wanted 'Las Vegas beauties in lavish costumes', but the girls wanted to play 'heavy, funky, show-type music'.[85] Finally, after touring the Pacific Northwest, East Asia and the rest of the United States in the late 1960s, The Pleasure Seekers disbanded and reformed as Cradle to begin exploring a harder rock sound.

Most all-girl garage bands faced the same issues as The Pleasure Seekers but on a smaller, more local scale. Just how many of these bands existed is hard to determine; Markesich lists 31 all-girl bands that released records, so they were certainly in the minority.[86] Some of the band names reflect a feminist consciousness – The Female Species, The Feminine Complex, Girls Take Over, She and The Virginia Wolves – and their recordings mainly fall into the category of pop-rock, with songs about boys and romance sung in the style of Motown girl groups like The Shirelles. Their playing tends to be less forceful and more rudimentary than that of their male counterparts, but there are exceptions, such as The Continental Co-ets, who were a popular live attraction at the teen fairs and clubs in the region and the only girl group from Minnesota to put out a record in the 1960s.[87] The B-side of their 1966 single 'Medley of Junk' is a rambunctious, tone-bending surf instrumental that quotes melodies from 'Mary Had a Little Lamb', 'Wipeout' and other well-known tunes. The A-side, 'I Don't Love You No More', starts off with a log-thumping drum intro and a cool guitar riff reminiscent of 'Hanky Panky'; after that, the song boasts minor-key chord changes, the complex interweaving of R&B guitar licks and smooth vocals. The strongest song in the canon of all-girl garage music is arguably The Belles' 'Melvin', a feminist parody of Van Morrison's 'Gloria' in which The Belles reverse the genders of the subject and the vocalist so that a girl is singing about how good the loving attention of a guy makes her feel. The song was meant to be a tribute to Melvin Bucci, the lead singer of another garage band from Florida named The Vandals,[88] but giving the lover a nerdy name like 'Melvin' instead of a sexy name like 'Gloria' makes the song seem like a satire of the well-known garage classic. Moreover, The Belles' singer delivers the words in an unabashed tough-girl voice and the band punches out the music with no frills, turning it into a bold garage-punk statement.

There were of course other all-girl groups that could hold their own. In 1966, Chicago's The Daughters of Eve released 'Don't Waste My Time', a defiant pop-rock song with the usual harmonized vocals that also boasts some powerful drum rolls, slashing guitar chords and nimble-fingered bass runs.[89] Another assertive pop-rock song is 'I'm Gonna Destroy That Boy' by The What Four, a band from New York City that released two 45s on Columbia Records.[90] 'Destroy That Boy' has typical harmonized voices singing about winning a boy's affections, but the piano-based song also includes some odd chord changes and unusual-sounding guitar technique. A song with a different approach to vocals is 'Hurtin Kind' by The Bittersweets, a group from Cleveland, Ohio.[91] In this folk-punker, the main vocalist sings solo in a throaty, low-pitched voice about a guy's treacherous ways while the backing vocalists sing ethereal, high-pitched 'oooo's from far off in the distance. Another group with a folk-rock sound was the Feebeez of Albuquerque, New Mexico.[92] 'Walk Away', the single they released in 1966, is a fast-paced folk-punk song with vocals sung in unison but also some tricky tempo changes that most male garage bands wouldn't have attempted. The flipside, 'Season Comes', has thick choral vocals sung over a slower, heavier, minor-key backing track. One final example is The Moppets, a group made up of four women who attended Mount Holyoke College in Massachusetts; they were in great demand at nearby men's colleges and carried their gear in a 1957 hearse, showing that all-girl garage groups could be just as colourful as their male counterparts.[93]

Garage Psych

The last major development in 1960s garage music was psychedelic rock, a style that uses sound to simulate the altered perceptions of someone who has taken a hallucinogenic drug. As Hicks explains, these effects include dechronization, which involves a distorted sense of the passing of time; depersonalization, which causes the user to lose his or her sense of self and have a feeling of merging with the cosmos; and dynamization, which causes static, solid objects to appear to bend, dissolve or move fluidly as if the world were made up of soft, mutable things.[94] First, acid rock simulates dechronization by slowing down song tempos and/or introducing long jams or aimless solos, along with extended introductions or codas.[95] Second, psychedelic musicians try to cause depersonalization in their listeners by playing at extremely high volumes; the loudness of the music literally vibrates the listeners' bodies and dissolves the barriers between them and the sound. Psych musicians also use large doses of reverb on their instruments or voices to approximate the sensation caused by LSD whereby sounds seem to be coming from far off or from inside a huge cavernous space, causing the listener to lose a sense of where the self is in relation to the sound.[96] Third, psychedelic music 'dynamizes' the auditory material of rock by using sound-effect devices such as vibrato arms, wah-wah pedals, fuzz boxes and phase-shifters to distort or alter the sounds made by guitars and other instruments. Tape effects such as echo and back-tracking, along with stereo panning and feedback, are also used to create hallucinatory sonic events. Moreover, psych musicians find ways to destabilize the harmony of songs by playing 'wrong' notes or chords, using more than one root chord in a composition and juxtaposing song parts that do not seem to belong together, thus suggesting the 'mind-bending' effects of LSD.[97]

After local musicians across the country heard the psychedelic sounds emanating from the West Coast and went on a few trips themselves, psychedelic qualities began showing up in garage music late in 1966. A textbook demonstration of the difference between straight garage rock and garage psych may be found in 1967's 'A Research into the Soul of Psychedelic Sound' by The Unbelievable Uglies of Minnesota. This song deconstructs a cover version of The Yardbirds' 'I'm a Man' and rearranges it while also radically altering its instrumental tracks to give an impression of how the song might sound to someone on an LSD trip. The piece begins with the ending – the grand finale at the very end of the rave-up that closes out 'I'm a Man'. Then someone utters the archetypal bratty taunt, 'Nyah, nyah, nyah, nyah, nyah', following the melody of a Yardbirds' guitar riff. Next, we hear the band play the main riff of 'I'm a Man', which fades out before the entire opening section is repeated in reverse. After the backtracking, the song jumps to the pseudo-double time section of the rave-up, where the band vamps on one chord and shifts into playing the much-parodied 'Cossack's dance'. Then we hear waves of guitar feedback before The Uglies play The Yardbirds' four-note descending riff over and over; this part slows down, speeds up to a climax, slows down again and then goes into the rave-up finale before fading out with guitar feedback. As difficult as it may be to enjoy, this piece provides a catalogue of psychedelic techniques and sounds in one three-minute tune; of course, one could also hear it as The Uglies' satire of psychedelic music and its excesses.

The psychedelic movement caused musicians to move away from playing music for dancing (body music) to music for introspective listening (head music), and rock bands began employing more psychedelic sounds along with lyrics that examine states of mind. One of the earliest and most successful garage-psych songs of this kind is 'I Had Too Much to Dream (Last Night)' by The Electric Prunes. It opens with a buzzing, wavering tone that grows in volume before some shimmering, liquid autoharp chords and a pulsating bass line come in. Then vocalist Jim Lowe sings about having a vision of a warm, intimate moment with his lover, whose hand reaches out to comfort him, only for him to wake up alone at dawn to realize that she was never there. His words emphasize the emptiness and loneliness of the room without her actual presence, suggesting the melancholy comedown at the end of an LSD trip. During the verses, the background music has the otherworldly, gossamer texture of a dream, being made up of autoharp chords and backtracked fuzz-guitar lines that sound like violins playing Middle Eastern melodies; however, on the choruses, the loud, pounding drums jar the listener back to the harshness of the here-and-now. A striking mixture of Stones-inspired garage punk, pop music and psychedelic experimentation, 'I Had Too Much to Dream' reached No. 11 in the pop charts in late 1966.

A darker examination of memory and the sadness of experience may be found in 'You Can't Erase a Mirror' by California's Children of the Mushroom. The song opens with a figure played on a church organ, followed by a slow series of arpeggios played on the guitar à la 'House of the Rising Sun'. The vocalist sings about looking back at his life and seeing missed opportunities, expressing regret that he can't change the things he has done. After the first verse, the lead guitar starts playing a double-tracked solo, with every line ending in undulating, howling feedback; as the song progresses, the guitar solos become increasingly sinister and haunting, with the feedback becoming more and more intense. Finally, the song ends with a church-organ flourish, leaving the listener in melancholy contemplation.

Otherwise, garage psych generally takes the form of songs about bad trips or songs that proselytize in favour of mind expansion and human evolution.[98] A classic example of a 'psycho-punk' song can be heard in 'Voices Green and Purple' by The Bees of Southern California. Dealing with the after-effects of an LSD trip, the song

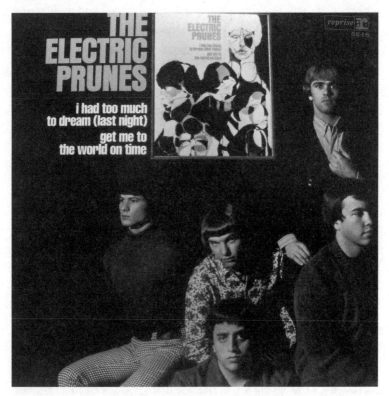

By blending otherworldly sounds with hard-rocking pop, The Electric Prunes created one of the first commercially successful psychedelic songs in 'I Had Too Much to Dream (Last Night)'.

opens with a fuzzy R&B riff being played at a fast clip while the vocalist talks about the voices he heard calling to him during the night. The song's persona is obviously suffering from drug-induced synaesthesia because he says that he *saw* the voices as green and purple shadows. Then the song shifts to the next section, where the guitarist plays chords that step up and down the fretboard in a mechanical, demented way and the drummer plays snare-drum rolls while the vocalist raves about the shadowy voices coming through the windows and climbing the walls to get him. Then he screams out 'Oh no, no!' in terror as the song fades. What makes this acid-punk gem so terrifying is the thought that flashbacks – the rebound effects of the hallucinogen – can come back to haunt the user at any time.[99]

Another acid-punk song that refers to drug-induced synaesthesia is 'Optical Sound' by The Human Expression, a Los Angeles band. Like 'Voices Green and Purple', this song uses a repetitive, mechanical beat as a trope for dementia; the drums play a reverberating click-clack beat that sounds like the ticking of a clock. A guitar plays a trebly arpeggio in time with the beat, while other guitar parts are mainly cries that slide up or down in pitch. Vocalist Jim Quarles sings in a tremulous, nasal voice about trying to reassemble his shattered mind as the sun rises. He seems to be looking around inside a torn-up room, for he says that he hates to think of what went on in there. To reinforce this image, the spacious, reverberant mix suggests the open space of a dark room. Other sounds, like the weird, warbling cry of a ghoul, punctuate the song as the persona describes looking into a mirror to see the image of a thought staring back at him. Songs such as these two indicate that not all garage bands embraced the idea of expanding their minds through the use of hallucinogens.

On the other end of the spectrum, some garage bands preached the virtues of reaching new heights of consciousness by taking hallucinogenic drugs. Foremost among these groups were The 13th Floor Elevators, a legendary band from Austin, Texas, that was the first to describe itself as psychedelic. Tommy Hall served as The Elevators' philosophical adviser in addition to playing electric jug with the group; he and his wife Clementine wrote most of the band's early material. Clementine also chose the band's name, which referred to the fact that most American buildings have no thirteenth floor and the idea that listeners could reach a new level of consciousness by riding up to the 'thirteenth floor' with The Elevators.[100] Essentially a rock 'n' roll band, The Elevators achieved their psychedelic sound through reverb, intense rhythms and the hooting of Hall's electric jug. For instance, their song 'Reverberation' is built around a killer R&B riff and a chugging beat that breaks into a gallop here and there. Vocalist Roky Erickson, who had a powerful, high-pitched R&B voice, addresses some individual and says that he is full of doubts and fear; if he could become experienced by tripping and leaving his old consciousness behind, he could find peace of mind.

Likewise, 'Tried to Hide' is a catchy rock 'n' roll song in which Erickson tells an individual that he has a fear of turning on as well as a fascination with it, but that he also lied about it, pretending to a knowledge of psychedelic experience that he doesn't have, using the right words to talk about it but only guessing what they mean. The highlights of this track include Hall's burbling jug and Erickson's soaring, primal screams. Another song, 'Roller Coaster', displays The Elevators' often melancholy sound, as the main part is a mid-tempo, minor-key riff played against an open string in a i-iv-v chord progression. Here, Erickson sings about the need for the listener to open up his mind and discover the new, evolving purpose to human existence. The Elevators' song lyrics, unlike those of so many other psychedelic bands, are meaningful and have some intellectual depth; they do not equate psychedelia with outlandish noises and surreal nonsense lyrics like most other bands. The Elevators also managed to release three high-quality studio albums and one pseudo-live album in their three years together, overcoming internal conflicts, drug busts, law-enforcement hassles, legal problems and drug-related unreliability before dissolving. Interestingly enough, The 13th Floor Elevators

This flyer for a psychedelic show at the Vulcan Gas Co. in Austin, Texas, features three of the state's finest psych outfits: The 13th Floor Elevators, The Conqueroo and Shiva's Headband. The *Winnie the Pooh* theme is an Austin tradition; every year, the city holds an Eeyore's Birthday Party in Pease Park.

were not the only band of their kind; Texas had the largest psychedelic scene in the country outside the West Coast, and the state's notable psych bands include Bubble Puppy, The Conqueroo, Fever Tree, The Golden Dawn, The Lemon Fog, The Headstones, The Red Crayola, The Remaining Few, Shiva's Headband and Zakary Thaks.

Regrettably, as psychedelia permeated youth culture of the late 1960s, other subgenres of garage rock began to degenerate and disappear. The prevalence of psychedelic rock caused local bands to play longer, more ponderous songs filled with meaningless guitar solos, as did the harder, heavier rock of Cream, Blue Cheer and The Jimi Hendrix Experience.[101] Established groups had to change with the times or risk becoming irrelevant; some bands, such as Paul Revere and the Raiders, became victims of their own success by being boxed into a certain style and sound due to their mass popularity, and young people with underground sensibilities came to see them as unhip. Besides that, the number of garage bands declined after 1967; local groups fell apart as musicians grew older and entered college, got married and started families, or were drafted for military service during the Vietnam War. To be sure, a number of homegrown bands out in the hinterlands would continue to play and record earlier styles of garage rock after 1968, and some into the early '70s, but these bands were isolated and hardly visible outside their own communities.[102]

Consequently, the golden age of garage rock was pretty much over by the Summer of Love in 1967, meaning that this vast outpouring of creativity lasted for only three years. During this time, many thousands of young people took part in making music that continues to delight listeners today with its power and charm. Just how many young musicians were involved would be difficult to estimate, but in his discography Markesich lists over 4,000 American groups that released 45s in the mid-'60s, and he leaves out bands that recorded straight pop, blues, instrumentals, surf/hot rod music and hippy rock.[103] Vernon Joynson does include groups of these kinds in *Fuzz, Acid and Flowers*, and his group listings number at least 5,700. Non-recording groups greatly outnumber those that recorded, so if we assume that four or five non-recording groups existed for every one that released a record, then the number of garage bands that existed in the mid-1960s could range from about 16,000 to 29,000 or even more. Whatever the actual number, it would be safe to argue that the world has never seen an artistic movement as large as 1960s garage rock, and that never before have so many people been active in a subculture devoted to making and enjoying music.

3

The World Beaters:
The British Invasion and the Beat
Heard 'Round the World

The first wave of the British Invasion took place when The Shadows, Britain's quintessential instrumental combo, had an incredible string of chart-topping hits in the early 1960s, before anyone had heard of The Beatles. People around the world – especially in Asia and Europe – were captivated by their melodious, toe-tapping tunes.[1] Many people took up playing the guitar because of The Shadows, and some even formed combos of their own to play 'Shadow music'. When Beatlemania struck, these combos became passé overnight; soon, nearly every detail of the Beatles phenomenon became replicated in cities around the world, with local musicians forming Fab Four-type bands and hordes of screaming girls treating them like superstars. In other words, the concept of the Fab Four behaved like a complex of memes, self-replicating units of cultural expression.[2] Thus a beat music craze spread around the entire globe like a viral infection, followed by a passion for British R&B as played by The Rolling Stones, The Yardbirds, The Kinks and The Pretty Things. After this second phase of the British Invasion, international garage bands could choose to play Liverpudlian beat music, or they could play hard R&B. To complicate matters, some of the hippest international bands looked to the American scene for authentic material to play, even though American garage bands were themselves caught up in the same pattern of imitating British models. However, most homegrown combos, from Denmark to

Uruguay to Singapore, stuck with imitating British bands because that was what they were exposed to.

Spain and Latin America

Beatlemania in Spain was kicked off when the cinemas began showing *A Hard Day's Night* (1964), and the film became so popular that the theme song rose to No. 1 in the Spanish charts several times in late 1964.[3] The subsequent Beatles craze gave rise to a number of copycat bands, the most notable being Los Brincos. The 'Spanish Beatles' dominated the Spanish charts in the mid-'60s but never broke out internationally;[4] that honour went to Los Bravos, a beat-influenced pop group that formed one night in a *discoteca* in 1965. Producer Alain Milhaud saw them in Madrid and then took them to London to record 'Black is Black', a huge international hit that no other Spanish band could equal. Los Bravos became the most popular act in Spain, and Spanish teenagers became hooked on beat music and other aspects of British Mod culture.[5] Mods were working-class youth in Britain who had a fetish for wearing smart clothes, and who danced to beat music in cellar clubs and discotheques while hopped up on pills.

Another Spanish garage band, Los Salvajes, decided to go directly to the source of Merseybeat by relocating to Germany in 1964; the manager of the Star-Club found the band too hick for Hamburg, so sent them out to play the surrounding towns. They came back wearing German versions of what London Mods were wearing, painting 'OLÉ' on their clothes in imitation of The Who's arrows and bull's-eyes. Los Salvajes ended up playing at the Star-Club alongside The Searchers, The Hollies, The Kinks and Manfred Mann as well as German bands such as The Rattles, returning to Barcelona as seasoned professionals and paragons of Mod fashion.[6] During their absence, another garage band called Los Cheyenes took over Barcelona. They covered songs by The Kinks and adopted the

93

crunchy stop-and-go guitar-chord sound of 'You Really Got Me' and 'Till the End of the Day', but they also played ordinary British R&B; one of their originals, 'Bla, Bla, Bla', has the exuberant Mod sound of Ronnie Woods's band The Birds. Moreover, Los Cheyenes grew their hair longer than normal and developed a wild stage act, tossing their guitars up into the air. For their first record, RCA gave them a flamenco-flavoured song, but the vocalist changed the rhythm so that it sounded more like a rock song.[7]

Across the Atlantic, young people in Mexico had been *rocanrolers* since Elvis had become a worldwide sensation, and Mexican bands had been playing *refritos* (meaning 'refried' or 'rehashed'), up-tempo versions of American rock 'n' roll hits.[8] When Beatlemania spilled over the U.S. border, Mexican youths took to beat music just as readily. One garage band that gave teenagers what they wanted was Los Dug Dug's, who first heard records by The Beatles while playing in Texas and became the first Mexican group to cover songs by the Fab Four.[9] They began playing strip clubs in Tijuana before working their way up to *cafés cantante* (music clubs) and moving to Mexico City in 1966 to play *fusile* (literally, 'to aim at', meaning as authentic as possible) covers of Beatles hits.[10] After developing a rabid following, Los Dug Dug's signed with RCA and cut ten singles, including covers of U.S. hits such as 'Hanky Panky' and 'California Dreaming'. In 1968, an American tourist was so impressed with their abilities that he became their manager and relocated them to New York City, where they cut some demos. Unfortunately, their manager was too stingy to pay $5,000 in union dues so that Los Dug Dug's could perform legally in the better clubs of Manhattan, so they went back home.[11] After becoming part of *La Onda*, the Mexican counter-culture, the band released a psych album, *Los Dug Dug's*, in 1971.[12]

Other important garage bands include Los Apson, which became Mexico's top band in 1965 by embracing the post-Beatles British Invasion sound and playing *fusiles* of the raucous R&B being put out by The Kinks and The Rolling Stones as well as American bands such as The Blues Magoos. Los Apson also enhanced their popularity by singing in English; the more sophisticated patrons of the *cafés cantante* in the cities wanted to hear authentic English versions of mid-'60s rock 'n' roll.[13] Los Ovnis (The UFOS), became one of the best cover bands in Mexico City, but by 1968 they had written enough original material to release an LP called *Hippies*. With song titles such as 'Mi Protesta' and 'Infinito', the album reflects the attitudes of the time,[14] and also illustrates the general pattern established by American and British garage bands, with the British Invasion sound dominating the mid-'60s and evolving into hard rock and psych by the end of the decade.

Down in South America, a Uruguayan Invasion took place in Argentina alongside the British one. This invasion began when four young men in Montevideo formed Los Shakers after seeing *A Hard Day's Night*.[15] Patterning themselves after The Beatles, the members of Los Shakers got mop top haircuts, wore black designer suits and played Beatles covers and catchy pop originals in local clubs until EMI/Odeon asked them to come to Buenos Aires to record. After putting out a couple of singles, they broke out with 'Rompan Todo' (Break It All), a classic beat song.[16] In addition, Los Shakers recorded Spanish-language versions of each new Beatles single for the Uruguayan and Argentine markets. Becoming a Beatles surrogate for the region like Los Brincos in Spain and The Easybeats in Australia, Los Shakers also toured Paraguay, Bolivia, Venezuela and Brazil. They enjoyed the same level of fame as their models, being hounded by mobs of screaming girls everywhere they went.[17] This phenomenon caused Argentine record labels to start signing bands merely because they were from Uruguay, resulting in the Uruguayan Invasion.[18] One such group was Los Mockers, who could imitate the sound of the early Rolling Stones without sounding like a complete rip-off. Most of their material was original and sung in English by Polo Pereira, who had a Jagger-like voice. After signing with EMI Argentina, Los Mockers released an LP and a few singles, but their records failed to sell very well and they disbanded in 1967.[19] EMI/Odeon even tried to generate a Los Shakers/Los Mockers rivalry in imitation of the Beatles/Stones rivalry, but the two bands were friendly with each other and the promotion fizzled out.[20] In spite of Los Mockers' lack of success at the time, they became well known to garage enthusiasts during the 1980s and '90s, and many listeners now consider them to be the best South American band of the '60s.[21]

The Uruguayan Invasion ended when Argentina developed its own musical identity. This process began with The Wild Cats, Argentina's first teenage rock 'n' roll combo. Formed in Rosario in 1964 by some young fans of The Beatles, The Rolling Stones and

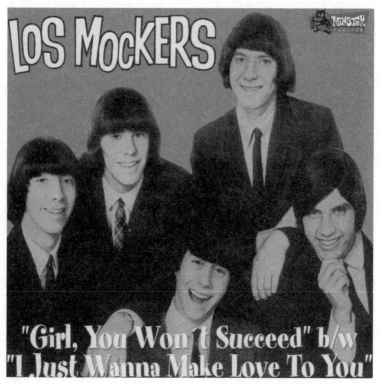

Picture sleeve for a single by Los Mockers, a band from Uruguay that was part of the Uruguayan Invasion of Argentina in the mid-1960s.

Los Gatos began as The Wild Cats, Argentina's first teenage rock 'n' roll combo, and their hit song 'La Balsa' helped to end the Uruguayan Invasion by establishing a market for records by native Argentinian bands.

The Yardbirds, The Cats took a nativist turn when they added a singer named Litto Nebbia to the group. Nebbia convinced his new bandmates to translate their name into Spanish and to begin singing in their native tongue. As Los Gatos Salvajes, the band moved to Buenos Aires and developed a following through television appearances. After releasing some singles and an LP in 1965, their record label went broke and Los Gatos Salvajes disbanded. However, Nebbia and one other bandmate stayed in Buenos Aires. They reformed the band as Los Gatos and sold over 200,000 copies of their debut single, 'La Balsa'.[22] This song seemed to express the mood of young people in Argentina at the time, and its popularity caused youth culture to blossom there, resulting in the growth of fanzines, independent record labels and music festivals. 'La Balsa' also served as an anthem for the hippy movement in Argentina, helping to set the stage for *rock nacional*.[23]

North of Argentina in Peru, the two most notable garage bands were influenced as much by American surf/instrumental rock as they were by the British Invasion. Los Saicos formed in 1964 in a middle-class district of Lima; they settled on their name because it reminded them of the Seiko watch as well as *Psycho*, Alfred Hitchcock's thriller.[24] Their most celebrated song is '¡Demolición!', a playful ditty about blowing up a railway station that became one of Peru's biggest radio hits in 1965.[25] Musically, the song is pure surf, with the main guitar riff being a I-IV-V progression played in the double-picking style of Dick Dale. What makes the song so arresting is Edwin Flores's gritty vocals; his voice is as guttural as a Tuvan throat singer's, and he punctuates the song with crazed-sounding yelps in addition to a line that goes 'TaTaTaTaTaTa Ya Ya Ya Ya', making it sound like the 'PaPaPaPaPaPa Mow Mow Papa' line in The Trashmen's 'Surfin' Bird'. Because of the anarchic craziness of '¡Demolición!', some people argue that Los Saicos 'invented' punk rock,[26] although The Sonics, The Velvet Underground and The Monks all have stronger claims on that territory. In truth, Los Saicos were no different from dozens of mid-'60s garage-punk bands in America that recorded slabs of rock 'n' roll insanity before moving on to other things.

The most accomplished garage band in Peru was Los Shain's, who formed in 1963 in the wealthiest district of Lima.[27] They could afford good equipment, playing Fender guitars, a Farfisa organ and Ludwig drums, and wore matching collarless jackets like those of The Beatles and The Trashmen.[28] Indeed, Los Shain's seemed to be well acquainted with Minneapolis's favourite rock 'n' rollers; not only did they record two Trashmen numbers for their first LP, *El Ritmo de Los Shain's* (1965), they also recorded a cover of 'The Crusher' by The Novas, calling it 'El Monstruo'.[29] Their interest in Los Trashmen was natural enough; 'Surfin' Bird' became a huge hit in Latin America, and the *Surfin' Bird* LP went gold in South America, leading to a Los Trashmen tour of the continent in 1965.[30] However, Los Shain's also covered such songs as Sam the Sham's 'Wooly Bully', The Seeds' 'Pushin' Too Hard' and The Yardbirds' version of 'Train Kept

A-Rollin".[31] Their best original is 'Shain's A Go Go', a mainly instrumental rocker with great guitar riffs punctuated by vocalist Gerardo Manuel's raucous, wigged-out utterances. They became a popular combo, touring the country and making television appearances; Los Shain's even appeared in a James Bond spoof called *Las Sicodelicas*.[32] After their first LP, Los Shain's followed the trends of the day, revealing the influence of the British Invasion on their second and third albums and becoming more psychedelic. Yet on their fourth and final LP before disbanding they put out another collection of instrumental rock,[33] leaving behind an impressive body of music for a local band.

Apart from countries where dictatorships suppressed rock 'n' roll, the beat movement led to garage bands springing up all over Latin America. An active beat scene emerged in Bogotá, Colombia, where the La Bomba nightclub had a rotating circular stage that swapped bands as one performance ended and another one began. La Bomba hosted the scene's best groups,[34] including Los Ampex and Los Young Beats, who dissolved and became The Time Machine, a dance band that began playing heavier rock. When the discotheques would no longer hire them, their guitarist and drummer left and joined the top band in Colombia, The Speakers.[35] The reformed Speakers put out two albums of South American-flavoured psychedelia; the last one, *En el Maravilloso Mundo de Ingeson* (1968), is considered a psych masterpiece.[36] One of the most experimental bands of the psych era was Os Mutantes, who formed in São Paulo, Brazil. Begun by two brothers, the band added a female singer and went through several permutations before settling on a line-up. After joining the Tropicália movement, which blended Brazilian culture with foreign influences in theatre, poetry and music, Os Mutantes put out their self-titled debut album, which mixes '60s pop songs with native folk music, jungle sounds, fuzz guitar, celestial choruses and studio effects.[37] A more conventional garage-psych band, Kaleidoscope, formed in the Dominican Republic and had two members from Puerto Rico. Orfeón, a Mexican record label, released only two hundred copies of the band's promotional album *Kaleidoscope*, which was once thought of as the 'mysterious crown jewel of Mexican Garage Psychedelia' because no one knew anything about the band for years.[38]

During the mid-'60s beat period in Venezuela, The Trashmen were bigger than The Beatles; 'Surfin' Bird' was the No. 1 hit on the radio for over four months, and when Los Trashmen toured the country, they appeared on *The Rene Show*, the Venezuelan equivalent of *The Ed Sullivan Show*. They also ran into a local group of devotees who called themselves Los Supersonicos and covered several Los Trashmen songs on their album. Los Supersonicos wanted to use the same brand-name equipment as their heroes but struggled to find it, so The Trashmen sold them all their gear when it was time to head back to the States.[39]

On the island of Puerto Rico, television producer Alfred D. Herger became the impresario of the local scene by presenting rock acts from the U.S. and the island to local viewers. Serving as the Ed Sullivan of Puerto Rico on shows such as *El Show del Medio Dia* and *La Discoteca Pepsi*, Herger ignited the 'Nueva Ola' (New Wave) movement, and in his view, the kings of the 'Modern Music wave' were The Sonsets (or The Sunsets).[40] On record, The Sonsets sound as gritty and hard-pounding as any stateside garage outfit, but Herger used the power of television to turn them into Puerto Rico's equivalent of The Beatles. In fact, one could say that television and film were essential elements in the spreading of 'Modern Music' throughout Latin America – radio airplay and popular magazine coverage alone would not have been strong enough to make Beatlemania and the British Invasion happen in Latin America.

Europe

Like everyone else in the world, young Europeans imbibed the intoxicating strains of Merseybeat and found them good, but they really went wild for British R&B, that revved-up take on African American rhythm and blues. British bands such as The Yardbirds, The Pretty Things and The Downliners Sect sped up American blues songs, creating forward momentum through a pounding beat and the frenzied strumming of rhythm guitars, exaggerating each song's rhythmic pulse and losing the gravitas and soulfulness it may have had in the original. Continental youth were exposed to this music through the touring of British bands and pirate radio stations set up off the coast of Britain.[41] These pirate stations sprang up on ships and in old sea forts along the British coast because the BBC gave very little airtime to pop music and entrepreneurs wanted to give young Britons the 'now' sounds they craved.[42] Many young people on the Continent heard these broadcasts as well, and, according to Greg Shaw, young Europeans took to the raw R&B of the Brits because of their need for an 'underground' music that had nothing to do with their own native (and square) traditions.[43] When Continental garage combos imitated their British mentors, they created such exotic caricatures of American blues and R&B that American neo-garage bands of the 1980s and '90s imitated *them.*

Of all the Eurobeat groups, Dutch bands sound the most competent and 'familiar' to American or British ears. One of the earliest and best of the *Nederbiet* groups was The Motions, who began playing Shadows-style instrumentals in 1963 as The Ricochets. After opening for The Rolling Stones at the Kurhaus in The Hague and seeing a British R&B group in action, The Ricochets updated their look and sound.[44] Early songs such as 'You Bother Me' and 'It's Gone' are built on punchy, bottom-heavy, full-chord riffs like those used by The Who or The Kinks, while their vocal melodies and harmonies come straight from Liverpool. On 'Be the Woman I Need', the band plays an urgent Bo Diddley knock-off that also sounds like The Pretty Things' 'Rosalyn', with booming bass, embellished strumming on the rhythm guitar and Beatleseque vocals. Their sound was also influenced by the Indonesian rock bands that existed in the Netherlands. The Dutch had colonized Indonesia, and when young people there emigrated to the Netherlands, some of them began playing a hybrid of American rock 'n' roll and instrumentals mixed with their own folk music. These Indo-rock bands put on professional shows, with the musicians decked out in tuxes and dancing in unison to the beat.[45] The Motions' bass player, Henk Smitskamp, had played for an Indo-rock band and their rhythms informed The Motions' sound, helping to explain why their songs were so popular in Japan, and Asia in general.[46] Closer to home, The Motions' first single, 'It's Gone', ignited the beat movement in The Hague and ironically helped to make Indo-rock obsolete. The Motions were popular and played all over the Netherlands, but misfortune struck when their main songwriter, Robbie van Leeuwen, left the group in 1967 to form Shocking Blue, who became an international sensation with their hit song 'Venus'.[47]

The Motions' biggest rivals were The Golden Earrings, who began in 1961 as two schoolboys who got together to play guitar. Soon they formed a combo called The Tornados, playing instrumentals by The Ventures and The Shadows. After Britain's own Tornados had a hit with 'Telstar' in 1962, the band changed its name to The Golden Earrings. By 1964 they had a singer and were covering songs by The Kinks and The Zombies. They began playing at the Houtrust complex, a beat hangout in The Hague, and released their first single, 'Please Go', in 1965. This record has a softer sound than that of The Motions, being more of a folk-pop song with acoustic guitar and harmonica, but pirate station Radio Veronica broke it out as a hit that made it to No. 10 in the Dutch charts. The band also released its debut LP, *Just Earrings*, in 1965.[48] After the group acquired singer Barry Hay from The Haigs in 1967, The Golden Earrings experimented with their sound until they developed into the hard-rock band that most people associate with their hit song 'Radar Love'. To date, the band now known as Golden Earring has released 25 studio albums and had thirty singles in the Dutch Top Ten, making them the most successful rock group ever from the Netherlands.[49]

The finest homegrown Dutch band of the 1960s was The Outsiders. Conceived by singer Wally Tax when he was eleven years old, The Outsiders had two sides – a raucous R&B side and a delicate folk-rock one – mainly because Tax's musical influences were his father and mother. His father collected records by African American artists, buying them from American sailors staying at a nearby seamen's hostel in Amsterdam, so Tax grew to love the blues music of Elmore James, Brownie McGee, Sonny Terry and Little Walter.[50] Tax's mother, a Ukrainian gypsy who met his father in a Nazi labour camp, listened to Russian folk music and opera.[51] These influences showed up later in the songwriting of Tax and guitarist Ronnie Splinter. By 1965 The Outsiders had developed well enough to hold down a steady gig at the Las Vegas Club, where the group primarily covered songs by British bands but also managed to slip in a few of their own.[52] Their first single was released in autumn 1965; the A-side is 'You Mistreat Me', a crude R&B number in the style of The Pretty Things, with stop/start motion, downward swoops on the guitar and a fast-tempo rave-up in the middle section, while the B-side is 'Sun's Going Down', a folk-rock song with a melancholy Russian folk melody, a primitive guitar solo and surf-style arpeggios on the guitar chords.[53] The single failed to set the Netherlands on fire, but it established The Outsiders as representatives of rebellious youth in Dutch society.[54] All told, The Outsiders recorded some fifty original songs, ending their time together with an innovative psych-punk album called CQ (1968).

Out of all the Dutch bands, Q65 came the closest to being downright punk. Coming out of a working-class district of The Hague, Q65 devoted themselves to blues and R&B; they derived their name

Picture sleeve for a single by The Outsiders, a prolific mid-'60s Dutch band. Before breaking up in 1968, The Outsiders recorded CQ, a psychedelic album that has more of a post-punk flavour than a 'flower power' sensibility.

from the song titles 'Suzie Q' and 'Route 66', changing the number to '65' to commemorate the year of their formation.[55] Their singer, Willem Bieler, was a wild man who electrified girls with his outrageous behaviour, and their shows often turned into melees that released the violent impulses of their followers. Bieler's 'coal pit' pronunciation of English made for some rough vocals, whereas their drummer, Jay Baar, was a closet literary type who could write fluent lyrics in English.[56] Baar's cynicism shows up in their two best originals, 'The Life I Live' and 'I Got Nightmares', which prefigure 1970s punk with their dissonant chord changes. Q65 also covered classic blues songs in a raggedy, semi-inept fashion, but they played with such relentless force that their versions are highly intoxicating; the best ones are 'Spoonful' and 'Down in the Bottom', both of which appear on their debut album, *Revolution* (1966). Their record executives considered the band members to be 'long-haired scum', but Q65 sold tons of records; in fact, *Revolution* sold more than 35,000 copies, going gold in the Netherlands and beating out new releases by The Rolling Stones, The Animals and The Troggs.[57] Unfortunately, Bieler's goon-like hectoring of their bass player, along with the band members' heavy drug use, led to Q65's demise;[58] nevertheless they stand as one of the best garage bands that the Netherlands produced in the 1960s.

Most rock fans believe that Germany was nothing more than an incubator for British beat music, but in reality the country was thriving with its own beat/R&B groups by the mid-'60s. While Hamburg was the most prevalent location, many more beat clubs existed in southern Germany, where rock 'n' roll germinated because of the American GIs stationed there.[59] One of the most well-known beat bands was The Lords, who began in 1959 as a skiffle group that played American folk and blues learned from Lonnie Donegan.[60] As a beat group, The Lords played an odd mix of songs, among them 'Greensleeves', 'Que Sera', 'Tobacco Road' and 'Shakin' All Over'.[61] They also dressed like aristocrats, sporting pageboy haircuts, tight-fitting suits, frilly shirts and pointy-toed shoes with spats. The Lords put on entertaining shows, but they had a lightweight sound. A much harder rock band was The Rattles, who could lay down a walloping *mach schau* (literally meaning 'make show!' but figuratively meaning 'let's go!') beat with the best of them. A cultural exchange programme with Britain made them as popular in Liverpool as the British beat bands were in Hamburg.[62] They were a good-natured, fun-time band that shook their Prince Valiant locks and smiled as they pounded

The Star-Club in Hamburg became a renowned centre for beat music after The Beatles played there for several weeks in 1962, but many American rock 'n' roll stars, such as Fats Domino, Bill Haley, Bo Diddley and Jerry Lee Lewis, also performed there.

out sing-along numbers such as 'La La La', 'Sha-La-La-La-La-Lee' and 'Come On and Sing', but The Rattles could also rock hard on songs such as 'Suzie Q' and 'Las Vegas'.

Most garage combos in Germany followed the pattern laid down by their American counterparts: some aspiring rock 'n' rollers meet in school and decide to form a band to escape the provincialism of their hometown. After learning how to play songs by The Rolling Stones, The Pretty Things and The Kinks, the combo gives itself a name and plays parties or teen clubs. Then the band begins competing in 'battles of the bands' (or 'beat festivals') and manages to record a single before breaking up. This pattern was followed by countless German teen combos, including The Loosers of Bad Oldesloe and The Tiles of Saarbrücken.[63] Germany's best garage band, The Boots, seemed to have a connection in the U.S., for they played American garage standards such as 'Gloria' and 'She's About a Mover' not long after the records were released. The Boots could also play with as much authority as the best American bands; their singer had a snarly, raspy voice, their guitarist often used a buzz-saw guitar tone and their drummer pounded the living hell out of his drums. Their panache is fully evident in the video for their performance of 'Gloria' on *Beat-Club*, the German music show: when the instrumental break comes up, the guitarist bends over, picks up an empty beer bottle from the stage and uses it as a slide to play his solo.

The most unique band on the German scene was actually made up of American servicemen from the army base in Gelnhausen. Initially calling themselves The Torquays, the ex-GIS played the beat circuit and became a popular good-time band. Around 1965, the bandmates grew bored with playing cover songs and began experimenting with distortion and feedback. They also began playing what they called an *Überbeat*, a simple, insistent rhythm. Bassist Eddie Shaw explains that they were after 'as much "bam-bam-bam-bam" on the beat' as possible.[64] Gary Burger, the guitarist/vocalist, also states that their new musical aesthetic was 'simplicity, repetitiveness, simple lyric lines, and don't make the song too long'.[65] Changing their image to go along with their 'overbeat minimalism',[66] the band renamed themselves The Monks and began wearing monk's robes, rope neck-ties and tonsured scalps. Their songs had titles such as 'Complications', 'Shut Up' and 'I Hate You'. Audiences either loved or hated them; sometimes the band members were physically attacked at shows by freaked-out workingmen.[67] However, The Monks became very popular in Hamburg because they were so different from the usual beat bands, and East Germans revered them because their bleak, alienated lyrics seem to address what was wrong with the world.[68] In 1966, Polydor released *Black Monk Time*, an album now regarded as a proto-punk classic, but the band's cynical views of war and romantic relationships were deemed too controversial by Polydor to be released in the u.s.,[69] so The Monks remained relatively unknown there until the 1990s.

The Swedes went as crazy for beat music as the Germans, with thousands of native bands springing up along with hundreds of nightclubs. In fact, the demand for beat music was so great that several British bands relocated to Sweden to leave the stiff competition at home behind. Many Swedish groups made records but they usually sold only a few; the local teens wanted to buy British records instead. In any case, the crucial step to success was being selected by jury to appear on *Tio i Topp*, a weekly radio programme for the Top Ten records. The most well-known Swedish bands include The Hep Stars, The Tages, Ola & The Janglers and The Shanes, with The Tages being the most accomplished.[70] The Tages began by imitating the Liverpudlian harmonies and bouncy rhythms of The Beatles and wearing sharp Mod clothes. They went on to play everything from raunchy R&B to mod-pop to psych-pop, becoming arguably as good as the best British bands.[71] The Shanes started off as raw R&B rockers in the mould of The Pretty Things; like most European garage bands, they did a raving version of Bo Diddley's 'Road Runner', but by 1967 they had settled down enough to release

'Chris Craft No. 9', a pop hit throughout Europe.[72] Another notable band is The Lee Kings, who recorded a song informed by The Who's 'My Generation' and 'Anyway Anyhow Anywhere' called 'On My Way', which stands as one of the greatest Swedish singles ever.[73] Perhaps the wildest bunch of all was the Lea Riders Group, who have been compared to The Mothers of Invention or The Deviants. Their first single was a primitive R&B raver called 'Got No Woman!', but their third single was recorded for a film about the Mod generation called *Dom Kallar Oss Mods* (They Call Us Misfits, 1968); the theme song by the Lea Riders is an intense acid-punk account of being 'a confused, dope-addled teenage failure'.[74]

It was probably combos like the Lea Riders Group that caused the mass media of Denmark to call beat groups *pigstradsorkestre*

The Monks, a group made up of American ex-servicemen, were one of the local bands that played the Star-Club in Hamburg. As *Überbeat* minimalists and proto-punks, they played up the monk gimmick by dressing in black, wearing rope neck-ties and sporting tonsured scalps.

(barbed wire bands); to their credit, Danish beat bands made *pig-stradmusik* and wore the label with pride. One of the country's most popular bands was The Lions, who formed in Copenhagen in 1963. A stylish, photogenic outfit, they mainly covered rock 'n' roll stand-ards such as 'Skinny Minnie', 'Sticks and Stones', 'Teenage Letter', 'Hippy Hippy Shake' and 'Shakin' All Over', but they also wrote a Merseybeat original called 'Hit House Shake' about the Copenhagen club they played. The best Danish beat band was Danny & The Royal Strings. Starting out as a Shadows-type instrumental combo, they were one of the first groups from outside Copenhagen to find national success. A couple of their members had extremely long hair for the time, and during 1965 and '66 they produced such outstand-ing examples of beat music as 'Come Right Back', 'Promise You'll Do' and 'Get Away'. Otherwise, the Danish scene was enriched by the work of Jack Fridthjof, who grew up overseas because of his father's job with an international aid organization. While living in Rome as a teenager, Fridthjof worked in a recording studio and pro-duced several records by The Rokes. After returning to Denmark, he opened a recording studio in Jutland and formed Jacks Beat Records, releasing records by many garage bands that had no chance of recording in Copenhagen. The bands that he recorded include The Snakes, The Rockets, The All Rounds, The Wiking Strings and Jack & The Outlaws, most of whom played standards such as the requisite 'Road Runner' and sang lyrics in dubious English. If not for Fridthjof, the music created by many such bands in Denmark would now be lost forever.[75]

The beat movement in Norway was similar to those in Denmark and Sweden. The most successful groups all went through a phase as 'Shadow bands' before imitating The Beatles. Of these, The Snapshots, The Vanguards, The Pussycats, The Cool Cats and 1-2-6 are the most recognized, with The Pussycats being the most influ-ential. Their *Pssst! Pssst!* album of 1966 was the best Norwegian rock album to date, and they followed it by recording a second LP,

Mrrr . . . Mrrr, in Hamburg that same year.[76] However, the most interesting Norwegian band was an all-girl group called The Dandy Girls. Formed in Hønefoss by lead guitarist Inger Tragethon, the group began by playing 'Shadow music' as well as covers of songs by British bands.[77] Record producer Thor Gunnar Norås heard about them and cast them in a movie called *Broder Gabrielsen* (1966); after that, Norås became their manager and prepared them for life on the road as professional musicians.[78] The Dandys recorded two 45s for the Manu label in 1966; one consisted of two instrumental numbers and the other one covered two Norwegian children's songs. Those would prove to be The Dandy Girls' only recordings, for they spent the rest of their time together on the road.

First, the band toured the military bases of Norway and Sweden in a Volkswagen van nicknamed 'Chaltrik'; they had fixed a horse's skull to the top of it, and their fans would write messages all over the van.[79] Word about this unusual beat band got around, so The Dandys toured Sweden and Switzerland next, driving a Chevy Bel-Air and pulling a travel trailer. In April 1967 they turned down an offer to open for The Rolling Stones in Zurich, mainly because the Stones demanded that the band pay for the privilege; Swiss groups The Sevens and Les Sauterelles opened for the Stones instead. Then Tragethon left the group to finish high school and was replaced by two Swiss musicians, Gaby from The Swiss Beat Girls and Rosemarie from The Ladies.[80] Throughout 1967 The Dandy Girls played all over Switzerland, Germany and Italy, often at high-end hotels and nightclubs. As pretty teenage girls who could rock and roll, they also became very popular at the military bases in Germany, where they often played for soldiers who had been wounded in the Vietnam conflict. As their reputation expanded, agents from Asia began calling for bookings, and their management set up a tour there.[81] Ultimately, The Dandy Girls won over audiences in Thailand, the Philippines, Indonesia, Malaysia, Japan and Iran, often by singing meaningful local songs in the native language in addition to their exuberant brand of rock 'n' roll. They were also supposed to tour Vietnam, but ultimately cancelled those dates because the war had intensified. By the end of 1968, The Dandys had had enough adventures; they returned home to Norway and Switzerland and called it a day.[82]

The beat scenes elsewhere in Europe were a mixed bag. On the one hand, Switzerland had a healthy response to beat music, with the aforementioned Sevens and Les Sauterelles being top-notch groups. At their best, both groups sound more American than British, with The Sevens delivering a heavy, punchy tune in 'What Can I Do' and Les Sauterelles sounding like an American garage-punk outfit on 'Spring Time' as well as their Bo Diddley pounder 'Janet'. On the other hand, France had an insipid response to the Big Beat; French bands had such a hard time rocking and rolling that most of their songs sound like off-the-wall lounge music. One exception is The Boots, whose 'Laissez Briller Le Soleil' is a stomping blues shuffle embellished with a wailing harmonica and several rave-up sections. Yet, like other French bands, The Boots insisted on singing in French, making their music less accessible to a wide audience.

The youth in Italy were so far behind the times that the first beat groups there were British émigrés who wanted to escape the competition back in Britain, including such groups as The Rokes, The Sorrows, The Renegades and The Primitives;[83] of these bands, The Rokes were the first to play R&B in Italy, bringing the sound of pre-Beatles Hamburg with them straight from the Star-Club. They also had the most success in Italy, having a hit with 'Piage Con Me', which later became a smash hit for The Grassroots as 'Let's Live for Today'.[84] Faring better than the Italians were the Greeks, whose garage bands were so naive and primal sounding that their music has an inescapable charm. An outstanding example is The Rabbits' 'I'm Looking in the Universe', a song that consists of a single two-chord riff and lyrics in which the singer tells a girl that by looking at signs in the universe, he can tell he will be a big shot one day.[85]

Australia and Oceania

Beatlemania among teenage girls in Australia reached fever-pitch in the mid-'60s, driven largely by the strong influence of Britain on the Land Down Under. Adelaide, Melbourne and Sydney were the centres for youth culture, with Melbourne being hipper than the larger but more conservative Sydney. Adelaide was by far the smallest city of the three, but it had the advantage of being close to Elizabeth, a town that was tailored to new incoming British migrants. In the 1960s Elizabeth was full of British youths who had recently seen The Dave Clark Five, The Beatles, The Rolling Stones and The Pretty Things, and these teenagers gave the bands in Adelaide tips on how to look, how to act onstage, which songs to play and so on, putting Adelaide groups on the cutting edge of British Invasion culture.[86] Consequently, some of the Adelaide bands were the best in the country, but they had to conquer Melbourne if they wanted to make it; the larger city had the rock magazines, the record label, the television stations and the radio stations to promote new records.[87] Moreover, Adelaide had no more than ten or fifteen discotheques, while Melbourne had about a hundred. Yet in both cities the demand for beat music was so great that a band could play three or four different clubs in one night. The discos were mainly dry, because no one under the age of 21 could drink alcohol, but kids flocked to the clubs because they wanted to dance to live music and socialize.[88]

The biggest band to come out of the Adelaide scene, and one that helped to forge the raw 'Australian sound', was The Masters Apprentices. Starting off as a Shadows-type instrumental combo called The Mustangs, the band changed direction when they took on singer Jim Keays, a young Scottish rock 'n' roller. Keays updated the other boys' wardrobes and got them into playing R&B and blues.[89] They renamed themselves The Masters Apprentices to acknowledge their debt to master bluesmen such as Lead Belly, Muddy Waters, Jimmy Reed and Bo Diddley. Soon, they were winning over audiences at The Beat Basement, a cellar venue like The Cavern Club, and The Octagon in Elizabeth, where the top Australian groups performed.[90] They recorded their first single in Melbourne in 1966, and it demonstrates the versatility and freshness of rhythm guitarist Mick Bower's songwriting: 'Undecided' has a grungy, Yardbirds-style riff that alternates with a Kinks-style rhythm part, while 'Wars or Hands of Time' is a minor-chord folk-rocker with a Merseybeat feel on the choruses. When 'Undecided' hit nationally, The Masters began playing fifteen gigs a week to hordes of screaming girls.[91] In 1967 the group recorded 'Living in a Child's Dream', a wistful bit of psych-pop that became a smash hit and showed off Bower's songwriting acumen once again. Unfortunately, playing three or four shows a night and being mobbed by clothes-ripping, star-struck girls took its toll;[92] their lead guitarist had to quit because of lung problems, and Bower left the group after he suffered a nervous breakdown. Indeed, The Masters went through so many line-up changes that Keays was the only original member who stayed on until the band's demise in England in the early 1970s. Since then, The Masters Apprentices have been recognized as one of the greatest groups in Australian rock during the 'scream era' – a period in the 1960s epitomized by teenage girls screaming through their idols' performances.[93]

However, the undisputed rulers of Australia's 'scream era' were The Easybeats, who came together at the Villawood Migrant Youth Hostel in Sydney.[94] Bassist Dick Diamonde and guitarist Harry Vanda came from the Netherlands, while guitarist George Young (the older brother of AC/DC's Malcolm and Angus Young) hailed from Scotland; singer Stevie Wright had migrated from Britain years earlier. Most importantly, drummer Snowy Fleet was born and raised in Liverpool and had played in The Mojos, so he brought his first-hand knowledge of Merseybeat to the group. The Easybeats had twenty original songs in hand when they signed to Australian EMI's Parlophone label, and their early records have the Liverpool sound; what made the group stand out was their enthusiasm and kinetic energy. Their second single, 'She's So Fine', reached No. 1 in the charts, and they produced eight Top Ten hits within a year and a half, becoming the kings of the Australian beat scene from 1965 onwards. Late in 1966, The Easybeats moved to Britain and had their first UK hit with 'Friday on My Mind', an infectious piece of beat-pop that reached the Top Ten in Britain and Europe and the Top Twenty in the U.S. The band's high point came when it returned to Australia for a triumphant national tour; after that, the Vanda/Young songwriting team began composing more complex psychedelic-flavoured pop, but the band became a shadow of its former self in live performances, and its songs degenerated into pleasant singalong music. The Easybeats made one last tour of Australia in 1969 and called it quits; Vanda and Young became full-time producers and songwriters, helping to put AC/DC on the road to stardom.[95]

The most notorious garage band in Australia was The Missing Links, a hard R&B outfit who turned heads on the streets of Sydney with their long hair and outré get-ups. Their first single, 'We 2 Should Live', became a No. 2 hit in New Zealand, but they broke up shortly afterwards.[96] Drummer Andy James and two other members re-formed the band, with James moving to vocals and congas.[97] This second line-up took a more experimental approach to R&B, often playing thirty-minute, feedback-laden versions of The Pretty Things' 'Mama Keep Your Big Mouth Shut', which also featured James banging on the conga drum with his mic to get a ringing tone. Crowds packed venues such as Suzie Wong's and Beatle Village in Kings Cross to watch James swing from the rafters and trash his bandmates' equipment, and Phillips signed them to a recording deal. Their best record is the raw but catchy garage-punk song 'Wild about You', which features clever lyrics, a string-scraping, rustling sound and ordinary feedback. 'You're Driving Me Insane' is a Kinks-style rocker with organ riffing and crazed guitar solos. On The Missing Links' debut album, Phillips included a backwards recording of 'Mama Keep Your Big Mouth Shut' called 'H'toum Tuhs' in an attempt to recreate The Missing Links' 'jungle/space' sound.[98] The LP also had several cover songs, including Bob Dylan's 'On the Road Again' and The Green Beans' '(Don't Give Me No) Friction', suggesting that the band was in touch with the U.S. garage scene. All told, the band released multiple singles, an EP and an LP, but their lack of commercial success caused them to fold, with guitarist Doug Ford eventually going on to join The Masters Apprentices.[99]

Even though The Beatles visited New Zealand in June of 1964, the beat movement there lagged behind Australia's because of the conservatism of New Zealand society and the lack of music-related infrastructure. Mike Rudd, vocalist and guitarist of Chants R&B, a group from Christchurch, explains that there was no music press and the only teen music on the radio was a weekly hit parade on the national station.[100] Just a few R&B groups existed there in 1965, among them Chants R&B, The Dark Ages in Auckland, and Bari and the Breakaways in Wellington.[101] However, by the end of the year, New Zealand's pop industry was booming, with new bands forming, record companies signing the best of them and fans buying home-grown records. In Auckland, R&B bands could play the Oriental Ballroom, 1480 Village, Galaxie and Monaco; the top beat club was The Platterack, where The La De Das became the house band by 1966. Patterning themselves after The Rolling Stones, The La De Das became the most popular band in New Zealand after having a hit with 'How Is the Air Up There?', a snotty fuzz-punk song by New York's The Changin' Times.[102] In truth, the best New Zealand garage band was Tom Thumb, who played loud, raucous shows at The Place and Ali Baba's and tried to live up to their image as the bad boys of Wellington. On their second single in 1967, Tom Thumb did a bang-up version of The 13th Floor Elevators' 'You're Gonna Miss Me';[103] their best original is 'I Need You', a Mod song built around punchy, resonant bass riffs. Nevertheless, despite rave reviews and appearances on television shows such as *C'mon* and *Happen Inn*, Tom Thumb failed to gain nationwide success.[104]

Elsewhere in Oceania, an exotic, homegrown rock 'n' roll blossomed. In Papua New Guinea, string bands playing American-style country music had been common since the early 1960s, with Rabaul in East New Britain becoming a centre for contemporary music. After it became legal for Papua New Guineans to drink alcohol in hotels and taverns, the first 'power bands' playing amplified rock 'n' roll emerged. Usually put together by young men with mixed European and indigenous origins, the earliest power bands formed around 1967. One of the first was The Freebeats, who had a passionate singer in the James Brown mould, and their soul-inflected song 'Midnight Mover' shows off his vocal machismo.[105] Perhaps the most accomplished power band was The Kopy Kats, who played Liverpool-style rock 'n' roll with strong harmony vocals, clean guitars and straightforward drumbeats. On songs such as 'Let Me Be' and 'Maryanne', one can hear echoes of The Everly Brothers and The Searchers. Another talented vocal group was The Stalemates, who played easy-going, melodic rock that sounds like The Ventures because of their clean guitar sound and basic drumbeats. Yet they sang in flawless English with dynamic, melodious voices; on 'Easy as Can Be', their main singer pushes his voice on the emotional parts to get a throaty, gritty tone.

The Papua New Guinea band most likely to be labelled 'garage' was The Kontikis, who covered such standards as 'Gloria' and '(I Can't Get No) Satisfaction'. They are more impressive on 'I'll Make You Mine', a beat song with effective build-ups and releases, infectious chord changes, cool guitar riffs and falsetto vocals. Such examples show once again that the British Invasion propagated American rock 'n' roll in the most culturally diverse corners of the world.

Asia

In Asia, homegrown rock 'n' roll bands formed wherever large num-bers of British or American military personnel were stationed. Not only did the troops expose locals to new forms of music, but ser-vicemen wanted to be entertained by live bands. In Singapore, for example, most bands played the British forces circuit; they would perform British-style rock 'n' roll at house parties or afternoon tea dances in addition to clubs. One club, the Golden Venus, hosted a Beat and Blues Session every Sunday afternoon, and the resident band there was The Checkmates. Following the usual pattern, The Checkmates started as an instrumental combo after The Shadows performed in Singapore in 1961 and electrified the local population. During the Beatles Invasion, The Checkmates got into vocal music by backing up pop singer Shirley Nair, but they normally played R&B instead of beat-pop.[106] Next, they backed up The Cyclones, a male singing duo, and took up the residency at the Golden Venus. Phillips signed the group and released their first EP, which included tuff instros such as '45 RPM' and 'Galaxy'.[107] After adding singer Vernon Cornelius to the line-up, The Checkmates became Unit 4 Plus 2 Plus 1.[108] An EP recorded with The Cyclones shows that they were way ahead of other Singapore bands at the time; both guitars play interwoven riffs instead of following the usual rhythm/lead guitar approach.[109] Their song 'Oh No, She Didn't Say' went to No. 1 in the Malaysian charts, and The Checkmates are credited with exposing Malaysian audiences to hard-driving R&B at a time when they were still enamoured of Shadows-style instrumentals.[110]

Before The Checkmates broke up in 1968, they passed their residency at the Golden Venus on to a more underground band, The Straydogs. Formed in 1966, The Straydogs played British R&B and blues at RAF circuit clubs and house parties.[111] One of their strengths was the harmonica playing of Ronnie Kriekenbeek, who helped to make their blues authentic, although they were sometimes required to play some 'off-beat' (cha-cha) dance music at certain clubs. After The Straydogs became the Golden Venus house band in 1967, they cut their first single, 'Mum's Too Pampering', backed with the American garage standard 'I Can Only Give You Everything'.[112] Their second single, 'Cold Morning', rose to No. 1 in the Malaysian charts in 1971, but The Straydogs still had the reputation of being a radical band because of their hardcore devotion to blues.[113]

To the north, in Hong Kong, the 'guitar band' scene exploded after The Beatles appeared at the Princess Theatre in 1964. Guitar bands formed with male lead singers instead of females and sang in English instead of Mandarin. Teen culture suddenly became visible in Hong Kong through tea dances, band competitions and concerts at Mong-kok Stadium, radio shows such as *Lucky Dip* and television shows such as Sam Hui's *Star Show*. The most ardent fans came out of the elite English-language schools, and the first guitar band to release a single, The Kontinentals, was formed by schoolboys at King George v School.[114] Their leader was Swedish bassist Anders Nelsson, who composed such hits as 'I Still Love You' and made The Kontinentals one of the top headliners in Hong Kong. Another top act was Danny Diaz and the Checkmates (a different band to Singapore's Check-mates), formed by three Filipino brothers with their brother-in-law. In fact, many musicians in Hong Kong were the offspring of Filipino immigrants. The Diaz brothers had a smash hit in 1966 with 'It's So Easy', and they had their big break when they won the Levi's Battle of the Bands at the Hong Kong Football Stadium in 1969.

However, the premier English-language band in the '60s was Teddy Robin and the Playboys, who had a huge hit with 'I Dreamed of You Last Night'. Other popular songs include the instrumental 'Sands of Time' as well as 'I Can't Grow Peaches on a Cherry Tree' and the psychedelic 'Magic Colours'. The Mystics, composed of young men of Portuguese descent, were popular at school parties and tea dances and introduced soul music to Hong Kong through numbers such as 'Sweet Soul Music' and 'Midnight Hour'.[115] Another important act in Hong Kong was The Quests, who were the most popular group in Singapore before taking 'Questmania!' with them to Hong Kong's Mocambo nightclub for two separate residencies. Three months after The Quests moved to Hong Kong, they had a No. 1 hit in the charts with 'Mr Rainbow'.[116]

Thai bands were not as slick or polished as the ones in Hong Kong, but they created a more eclectic form of guitar-based rock. People in Thailand were as smitten by The Shadows' instrumental tunes as everyone else in Asia and Europe, so Thai groups began playing 'Shadow music' too. Yet Thais were also exposed to the sounds of Elvis Presley, The Ventures, The Beatles and other big-name acts of the day through the presence of American military personnel brought to the region by the Vietnam War. In Bangkok, nightclubs and hotel lounges tried to cater to foreign tastes by providing 'string bands' that could play various styles of Western pop music.[117] As a result, local bands often gave traditional Thai melodies the 'Shadow' treatment or incorporated the sounds of surf guitar, rock 'n' roll, soul, blues or exotica into their music.[118] Such hybridization can be heard in the band Johnny Guitar, the self-appointed 'King of String Bands', which was led by organist T. Noparatana.[119] In their first hit, 'Suphan-nahong', one hears the melody from a song traditionally reserved for a ceremonial boat procession, accompanied by indigenous percussion in addition to electric guitar and organ.[120] In 'Bangsaen '66', a song about a beach resort near Bangkok, a screechy, Telstar-like organ trades riffs with a Ventures-style surf guitar.[121] The most celebrated composer of 'Thai Modernized Music' was Payong Mukda, who performed under various aliases.[122] Singing in Thai, he covered Little Richard's 'Lucille' as 'Loomsiah' and Ray Charles's 'What I'd Say' as 'Tamai Dern Sae'. With his group The Son of P.M., Mukda also recorded 'Boongatanyon', a rumba in which a vibraphone plays the melody and a surf guitar accents the rhythm. The Son of P.M. also recorded a woozy version of the 'James Bond Theme', adding an organ and native percussion instruments to the mix. A more Westernized band was The Cat, who tended to play a-go-go rock – a form of dance-orientated rock 'n' roll. Their rambunctious version of 'Do the Watusi' was the title track for their LP; they also created a mash-up of 'Jailhouse Rock' and 'Do the Watusi' called 'Jailhouse Watusi'.[123] Working with female singers, The Cat recorded a cute but subdued garage-rock song called 'Meow' as well as an energetic take on 'Hit the Road Jack'. Another recording that would have been typical of the music played in Bangkok nightspots is Vichan Maneechot's 'Dance Dance Dance', a Kinks-style number that got people moving with its distorted chords and stop-and-go rhythm.

Japan is another Asian country where the influences were as much American as British. The sensibilities of Japanese youths were inflamed by The Ventures, the American instrumental combo from Seattle that had its first hit in 1960 with 'Walk, Don't Run'. Of the 100 million records The Ventures have sold worldwide, 40 million were bought in Japan, and Ventures records have outsold Beatles records there by two to one. While the Fab Four did have some cultural impact on Japan, it was The Ventures' first tour in 1962 that caused Japanese youths to start playing electric guitars; The Ventures' sleek Fender guitars suggested 'modernity and sex' to Japanese teenagers, and the '*eleki* boom' (electric guitar boom) resulted.[124] Japan's answer to The Ventures was guitarist Takeshi Terauchi (known as Terry), who played in a fiery style and made liberal use of the vibrato bar. In the early '60s, Terry recorded guitar-based instrumentals with The Blue Jeans, but after the Beatles Invasion ushered in the more vocally orientated 'Group Sounds' (GS) movement he left the group to form The Bunnys, who performed everything from 'Irrevocable Vow', a slow, '50s-style vocal number, to 'Burning Burning', a hard-stomping tune with frenetic guitar solos and vocals in Japanese, along with moans and yelps.[125] The Bunnys' first single, 'Terry's Theme' backed with 'Test Driver', sounds harmonically and rhythmically as if it could have

The Spiders were the top Group Sounds band in Japan; they are pictured here in the Netherlands during their tour of Europe in the mid-1960s.

been recorded by The Ventures, but their best instrumental, 'Moanin'', has an intensity The Ventures never mustered, with ferocious R&B riffs, crazed guitar picking and vibrato-arm freak-outs.

Some of the best-known Group Sounds bands include The Tigers, The Wild Ones, The Golden Cups, The Tempters and The Mops, with the premier GS band being The Spiders. Working as an *eleki* band in the early '60s, The Spiders recorded such instrumentals as 'Wipeout' and 'Dynamite'. After adding singer Jun Inoue to their line-up in 1964, they evolved into a GS band and veered towards British R&B.[126] Their frenzied performances, combined with their dancing and goofing around onstage, set them apart from their GS contemporaries, and The Spiders were often asked to open shows for foreign groups such as The Ventures, The Astronauts and The Beach Boys. They wore matching suits (like The Beatles) and starred in four movies based on *Help!* (1965), the first one being *Wild Scheme A-Go-Go* (1967). Their debut *Album No. 1* contained all original material, while their *Album No. 2* consisted of cover songs. In an attempt to break out internationally, The Spiders played shows in the U.S. and Europe, even appearing on the British television show *Ready Steady Go!*, but their Japanese brand of R&B had only a small impact on the Western world.[127] At any rate, the tale of The Spiders' attempt to 'invade' the very countries from whence rock 'n' roll originated brings the story full circle. The British Invasion caused homegrown bands to spring up around the globe, fulfilling a universal need of youngsters everywhere to rock and roll regardless of their cultural origins.

4

The Resurrectors: Bringing 1960s Garage Rock Back from the Grave in the 1970s

The only American garage band of any note to survive the 1960s intact, change with the times and thrive in the '70s was the Alice Cooper group, and their story shows how rock music evolved during that time.[1] Alice Cooper began life in Phoenix, Arizona, when a bunch of guys on the cross-country track team at Cortez High School put together a Beatles spoof for a talent show. Calling themselves The Earwigs, the five boys took the stage wearing mop top wigs and mimed their way through some Beatles songs.[2] The core members of The Earwigs enjoyed this foray into show business so much that they re-formed as a real band called The Spiders, with Vince Furnier on vocals, Glen Buxton on lead guitar, Dennis Dunaway on bass, John Tatum on rhythm guitar and John Super on drums. Playing British-style R&B of the kind purveyed by The Who and The Yardbirds, The Spiders released a decent single in 1965 called 'Why Don't You Love Me' and an outstanding one in 1966 called 'Don't Blow Your Mind'.[3] The latter song made it to No. 2 in the Tucson radio charts, and The Spiders developed a strong local following.[4] After jumping on the psych-wagon during 1967, the band changed its name to The Nazz and began playing more free-form, experimental rock. After venturing to Los Angeles for shows, The Nazz relocated to Santa Monica and finalized their line-up with Michael Bruce on rhythm guitar and Neal Smith on drums.[5] In Los Angeles, the bandmates immersed themselves in the counter-cultural milieu on Sunset Strip, dressing up in women's thrift-store clothing. The Nazz also became the house band for a while at the Cheetah club, where they enlivened their shows by hammering watermelons apart and blowing feathers out of pillows with carbon dioxide.[6]

By March 1968 the band had become Alice Cooper,[7] and a friendship with Christine of The GTOs led to an audition with Frank Zappa. Impressed by their offbeat material, Zappa signed the band to a three-album recording contract with Straight Records,[8] a deal that reflects the shift in rock music away from singles to long-playing albums as the main vehicle for selling music. The band's first album, *Pretties for You* (1969), consisted of avant-garde psychedelia; the second one, *Easy Action* (1970), featured more conventional rock songs, but it sold even fewer copies than the first. Before *Pretties* was even released, the group decided that they were too weird for Southern California and relocated to Detroit, where they joined the revved-up hard-rock scene there and played alongside MC5 and The Stooges.[9] Alice Cooper also played several outdoor festivals in 1969 and 1970, thus participating in another trend in rock music that involved larger and larger shows being held in arenas or stadiums. Meanwhile, Warner Bros bought Straight Records (including Alice Cooper's contract), and Bob Ezrin of Nimbus 9 Productions produced their third album, *Love It to Death* (1971).

Ezrin helped the band develop a harder-hitting yet more commercial sound;[10] subsequently, *Love It to Death* charted in the Billboard 200, and the single from this album, 'I'm Eighteen', became a smash hit, catapulting Alice Cooper from obscurity to public acclaim. The band's stage show also became increasingly theatrical, with the members wearing androgynous glam outfits and Furnier's 'Alice' persona being punished for his/her transgressions; the show climaxed with Alice being executed in a mock electric chair. With each successive album of the '70s selling more copies than the previous one, Alice Cooper's live show became more elaborate; when the band's popularity peaked after the release of *Billion Dollar Babies* (1973), their show had grown into a violent, macabre extravaganza that used numerous props and morality-driven set pieces.

The story of Alice Cooper shows just how quickly garage rock was left behind and forgotten as rock music evolved. In essence, the rise of Alice Cooper coincided with the development of arena rock, and the band's increasingly spectacular and outrageous shows reveal some of the excesses of the 1970s. As groups playing heavy blues-rock, hard rock or progressive rock performed for larger and larger audiences, the venues became bigger, the stage productions more elaborate and the playing of instruments – especially guitars – showier or flashier. Moreover, such bands also became more dependent on technical wizardry in the recording studio to create complex sounds that few musicians could recreate at home. As a result, the distance between rock stars and their audiences increased.[11] Not all fans were thrilled by the 'bigger is better' mentality of corporate rock; to some, the spirit of rock 'n' roll seemed to be missing from all this bombast. Such fans found even less satisfaction in other parts of the pop-music landscape: in one direction was the soft pop-rock of Elton John, The Carpenters and Bread; in another was the teenybopper pop of The Jackson 5 and The Osmonds; in yet another was the soporific crooning of singer-songwriters such as James Taylor, Carole King and Carly Simon. None of this pop music seemed designed as something to dance to.

The only glimmers of hope for fans of rock 'n' roll came from glam rock, a genre in which cross-dressing performers played back-to-basics rock. On the one hand, glam rockers focused on fashion and camp performance, wearing make-up, platform-soled boots and clothing made of shiny, space-age fabric, all of which suggested a futuristic androgyny; on the other, they played a retro form of rock that was good for dancing and having fun. Even the most sophisticated practitioners of glam, namely David Bowie and Roxy Music, fell back on the patterns and tropes of rock 'n' roll for many of their songs. The most influential glam band in America, the New York Dolls, adhered even more closely to the basic formula of rock 'n' roll. Serving as a mutant Rolling Stones for the 'Me Decade', with singer David Johansen playing the role of Mick Jagger and guitarist Johnny Thunders as Keith Richards, the Dolls' music drew heavily on rhythm and blues like that of The Stones, and the group covered such R&B classics as The Jayhawks' 'Stranded in the Jungle', Sonny Boy Williamson's 'Don't Start Me Talkin'' and Bo Diddley's 'Pills' in their own ramshackle style. Virtually every one of their originals, including 'Personality Crisis', 'Lookin' for a Kiss', 'Trash', Bad Girl' and 'Who Are the Mystery Girls?', uses the blues-guitar shuffle rhythm associated with Jimmy Reed and Chuck Berry, and most of Thunders' guitar solos are howling Chuck Berry-type licks. That said, the Dolls' songs do get away from the standard I-IV-V chord progressions of traditional rock 'n' roll, sometimes even using dissonant chord changes that would later play a huge part in the sound of punk. For this reason, in addition to their obnoxious, streetwise attitude, the Dolls are often seen as proto-punkers who were ahead of their time.[12] Yet as hard as the Dolls' music rocked and rolled, many rock fans couldn't get into their trashy streetwalker looks and campy posturing, so they never became more than a cult band. Besides that, the recorded output of the New York Dolls and the other glam groups was too small to keep rock 'n' roll fans satisfied for long.

During this time of discontent, a number of record collectors, fanzine writers and rock critics kept hope alive by discussing their love of rock 'n' roll among themselves. Before long, the idea of looking back at the rock music played by teen bands in the mid-1960s came up. One of the first to broach this idea was Greg Shaw, a fanzine publisher who would go on to become a giant in the world of garage rock. Born in San Francisco in 1949, Shaw got his start as a science fiction and fantasy fan. After acquiring a mimeograph machine as a youngster, he began publishing fanzines devoted to science fiction and the works of J.R.R. Tolkien. In the mid-1960s, a schoolmate named David Harris got him interested in covering rock music, and the two began publishing *Mojo Navigator*, a newsletter for the Bay Area music scene. This zine included interviews with bands such as Country Joe and the Fish, the Blues Magoos, the Grateful Dead and The Doors. In 1970, Shaw began publishing *Who Put the Bomp*, a zine named after Barry Mann's 1961 hit song. As the first self-styled 'rock fanzine', *WPTB* focused on 1950s rock 'n' roll,[13] but a turning point came in spring 1971, when issue 6 included an essay by Shaw called 'Prelude to the Morning of an Inventory of the '60s'. Here, Shaw proposed to drop his exploration of '50s rock 'n' roll, mainly because it had already been thoroughly catalogued and celebrated, and to look at the so-called 'golden age of rock' from 1963 to 1966. He wanted to begin with surf music because it was 'an indigenous music [that] arose to meet the cultural needs of a teenage scene'.[14] He then planned to move on to the American groups

GREG SHAW

Promo photo of Greg Shaw, an obsessive publisher of fanzines, astute historian of popular music and vigorous promoter of '60s garage rock.

that mushroomed after the British Invasion, listing The Remains, The Shadows of Knight, The Knickerbockers, The Outsiders, The Beau Brummels and many others. Next, Shaw mentioned the San Jose, California, groups inspired by The Who and The Yardbirds, including Count Five, The Syndicate of Sound, The Chocolate Watchband and so on. He argued that while 'most of this music was pretty bad compared to the rock & roll of the fifties . . . a lot of it was good in its own way and it deserves more attention than it's gotten so far'.[15] Shaw would sing a different tune later when he became a vigorous promoter of '60s garage rock, but in 1971 he was still feeling his way through new musical territory.

This issue of WPTB contains several other remarkable items, one being the announcement that Lenny Kaye was hard at work compiling a series of albums for Elektra Records that would revive forgotten singles from the mid- to late 1960s. The plan was to have each album focus on a regional music scene from that period. Shaw admits in another article that he is relieved by this news because he was about to suggest releasing a series of bootleg albums with the same theme.[16] As will be discussed later, the album that came out of Kaye's efforts would play a huge role in defining and reviving 1960s garage rock. Another remarkable feature of issue 6 is the pile of letters from big names in rock journalism; the correspondents include John Kreidl, Greil Marcus, Dave Marsh, Lenny Kaye, Charlie Gillett and Lester Bangs. The most thought-provoking letter of all comes from rock critic Marsh, who praises WPTB for helping to keep alive an 'underground cult' devoted to rock music. He describes the cultists as 'people who have a true aesthetic of raunch, a true love for high energy, gutlevel intensity in music', and he believes that such fans comprise 'a cult on the order of the Rosicrucians'. Then Marsh jokes that he and his fellow enthusiasts could promote rock 'n' roll by turning unenlightened people on to the esoteric 'secret of sound'.[17] Not only does Marsh's letter reveal how he and other fans of 'authentic' or 'genuine' rock 'n' roll saw themselves in relation to the larger body of mainstream consumers of rock, it also suggests that Marsh and his fellow enthusiasts should evangelize to the masses.

The showiest and most enthusiastic proselytizer of all was Lester Bangs, a rock critic who got his start by writing album reviews for *Rolling Stone*. Bangs absorbed the spontaneous, earthy writing of the Beats and produced his own kind of gonzo journalism; he would adopt eccentric personas and use their voices to air his own musical views. He produced two seminal essays in the early 1970s, one being 'James Taylor Marked for Death', a rant against the anodyne aesthetic of Taylor and his ilk as well as a tribute to The Troggs, Britain's premier garage band. This essay appeared in the Winter/Spring 1971 issue of *WPTB*, while his other masterpiece, 'Psychotic Reactions and Carburetor Dung: A Tale of Our Times', appeared in the June 1971 issue of *Creem*. Pretending to be a grandfather dandling his grandkids on his knees, Bangs proceeds to tell them, of all things, about the greatness of The Yardbirds, but he quickly digresses to the subject of their imitators, especially Count Five. Grandad Bangs tells the kids that we entered a 'mighty sad downer stretch' around 1970, when 'wandering minstrels and balladic bards' began singing such drivel as 'Why is there war well go ask the children they know everything we need to know'.[18] Nonsense of that kind drove him back to the 'good old '66 goof squat rock' played by bands like Count Five.[19] He admits that Count Five's 'Psychotic Reaction' is a real 'shlockhouse grinder', an inept imitation of The Yardbirds' 'I'm a Man', but he also claims that it is 'absolute dynamite', the perfect antidote to 'drowning in the kitschvats of Elton John and James Taylor'.[20] Grandad Bangs also makes light of Led Zeppelin and recalls that he bought Count Five's *Psychotic Reaction* album at the same time as The Who's *Happy Jack*, and he ended up listening to the former far more often, hopping and stomping in joy around the turntable as it played.[21] In essence, the central question that Bangs grapples with as he purportedly talks to his grandchildren

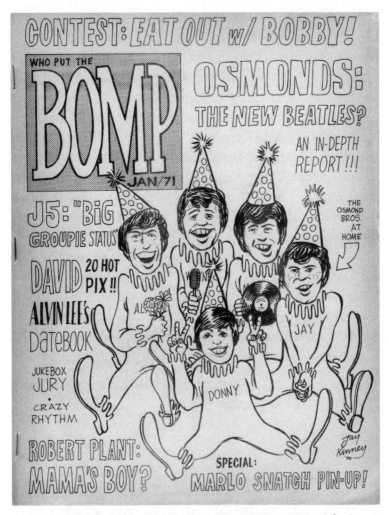

This issue of *Who Put the Bomp* represents a turning point in rock fandom, during which Greg Shaw and other rock enthusiasts talked about resurrecting teen rock 'n' roll combos of the mid-1960s from oblivion.

is this: Why should we listen to the barbaric bashing of 'little Teeno bands' or teen 'punk bands' when we can listen to the more professional sounds of The Yardbirds instead?[22] His answer is that 'grossness [is] the truest criterion for rock 'n' roll' and that 'the cruder the clang and grind, the more fun' it will be to listen to.[23]

131

Becoming reflective, Grandad Bangs goes on to say that the purpose of listening to recorded music is to experience that 'priceless moment' that one will remember all one's life, comparable to one's first orgasm, and in the end he concludes that Count Five were just as important as The Yardbirds in their own way, but that some artists are recognized in their own time while others are not.[24]

As entertaining as Bangs's writing could be, he had a hard time convincing the average Led Zeppelin or Jimi Hendrix fan to start listening to music from a quaint, bygone era (albeit one only five or six years in the past!). Besides that, unless a teenager had an older brother or sister with a good record collection, he or she would have had to dig around to find records from the 1960s anyway. That situation changed when *Nuggets: Original Artyfacts from the First Psychedelic Era, 1965–1968* was released by Elektra in 1972. The idea for *Nuggets* first came to Jac Holzman, the founder of Elektra Records and the man who signed such acts as MC5, The Stooges and The Doors to the label. Holzman found himself wondering what had happened to all those bands that had created one or two great tracks

The Troggs, one of the '60s bands that gave Lester Bangs a reason for hope, inspired many American bands to play primal, troglodytic rock.

during the '60s and then disappeared. He thought that a collection of such songs might have some appeal, so he cast about for an expert to put the project together and came up with Lenny Kaye.[25] Not only did Kaye work at the Village Oldies record store in New York, he also wrote music reviews for *Jazz and Pop* magazine as well as *Fusion*, *Crawdaddy* and *Rolling Stone*.[26] On top of that, Kaye had been a garage musician himself, playing guitar for The Zoo, a mid-'60s band that had played the college frat circuit from New York to Pennsylvania.[27] Kaye readily agreed to put *Nuggets* together and went to work. Originally, Holzman and Kaye planned to put out a series of albums tied to different regions, but licensing the songs for re-release proved to be so time-consuming and expensive that the two gave up and settled for a double-album compilation with 27 songs.[28]

These 27 nuggets of musical gold touch on nearly every style or mood of mid-'60s rock, ranging from garage psych and Stones-flavoured R&B punk to homemade pop. Over half of the singles spent time in the Top 100 charts, many making it to the Top Twenty, and the selection includes such classics as Count Five's 'Psychotic Reaction', The Electric Prunes' 'I Had Too Much to Dream (Last Night)', The Leaves' 'Hey Joe', The 13th Floor Elevators' 'You're Gonna Miss Me' and The Castaways' 'Liar Liar'. Kaye chose these songs not because they have the stereotypical 'fuzztone guitar and Farfisa organ' sound of the 1960s, but because he thought they were 'incredibly well-crafted and well-performed' songs.[29] As great as they are, these songs had pretty much been forgotten by 1972, and most up-and-coming teenagers of that decade had never heard of them. Not surprisingly, very few copies of *Nuggets* sold and it ended up in record cut-out bins within a year or so of being released.[30] Yet the album evidently reached the right people, for members of such well-known groups as R.E.M., Talking Heads and the Ramones have named it as a major influence. In fact, the album is often mentioned along with the work of The Stooges and The Velvet Underground as one of the main progenitors of punk and New Wave, genres encompassed by the New Wave movement.[31] Although *Nuggets* did help to instigate New Wave, it also found an audience among fans who were already on the verge of becoming punk rockers and New Wavers; sales of *Nuggets* tripled in 1976 when it was re-released by Sire Records, suggesting that the do-it-yourself sounds of *Nuggets* helped to satisfy an appetite that was already there at the birth of the New Wave.[32]

Of course, many other people helped to spur this movement along; in addition to the rock critics already mentioned, a number of record collectors and fanzine publishers worked endlessly to raise awareness of forgotten '60s music. One influential collector was Hans Kesteloo, a Dutch native who began collecting records by European bands in 1965. After trading singles with an American collector in Pennsylvania, Kesteloo was turned on to the glories of American garage music. He then began travelling to the u.s. about three times a year to scour record stores, thrift shops and flea markets. Before people such as Greg Shaw even began thinking about '60s records, Kesteloo had accumulated thousands of 45s. In the mid-1970s he began releasing the best of these songs on a series of compilation tapes called *The Never-ending Trip*. This 35-volume series helped to expose a large network of American collectors to singles that had been recorded by American bands during the 1960s.[33]

Down in Austin, Texas, two record collectors named David Shutt and Doug Hanners became dealers in the mid-1970s and began offering lists of obscure 45s and LPs for sale by mail order. They created the first 'state-themed' lists for punk and psych records from Texas, and they also rated the musical quality of their records by ranking them from one to four. These lists led to Shutt and Hanners compiling the first discography of obscure Texas recordings, *Journey to Tyme*.[34] Moreover, Hanners began publishing a fanzine devoted to Texas music, *Not Fade Away*, putting out four issues from 1975 to 1985. These fanzines were chock-full of stories about Texas bands and performers, along with photos and discographies. Similarly,

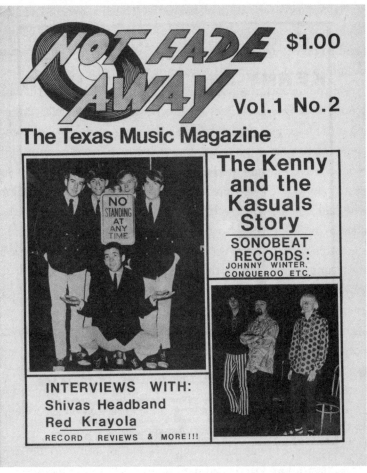

Not only did Texas produce more than its share of garage bands during the 1960s, but it had a large number of garage-rock fans during the 1970s and '80s. Doug Hanners and his fanzine *Not Fade Away* helped to generate that enthusiasm.

an enthusiast out in Los Angeles named Mark Shipper published *Flash*, a fanzine that included a 'Punk-rock Top Ten' of early '60s records in the June 1972 issue. Shortly before curating a compilation of The Sonics' material called *Explosives* in 1973,[35] Shipper convinced two friends to form a band devoted to reviving '60s garage rock.[36] Called The Droogs, the band released its first single in 1973, a cover of The Sonics' 'He's Waiting', backed by The Shadows of Knight's 'Light Bulb Blues'. Thus The Droogs became the first '70s garage band to revisit '60s music consciously, and they would go on to become part of the garage-revival movement of the '80s.[37]

In the meantime, another kind of band arose during the late 1960s and early '70s. Harking back to '60s garage rock while venturing into new musical territory, these bands played what has come to be called proto-punk. The musicians involved were not part of a cohesive movement and had no awareness of themselves as proto-punks, but they were conscious of themselves as outsiders who had no chance of receiving radio airplay. They resisted the dictates of the 'peace and love' generation and their songs expressed alienation while examining taboo subject-matter. To a large degree, these musicians derived their aesthetic sensibilities from The Velvet Underground, with their stripped-down, unpolished rock 'n' roll and experiments in feedback and distortion.[38] The Velvets also created songs too long and raucous for AM radio play, and Lou Reed's lyrics dwelt on the seamy experiences of transvestites and drug addicts. To a lesser degree, The Sonics served as another predecessor for proto-punk bands; not only did they play in a raw, aggressive manner, but their lyrics in 'The Witch', 'Psycho' and 'Strychnine' dealt with offbeat or unwholesome subjects.

In response to this mix of influences and conditions in the early 1970s, proto-punk bands sprouted up throughout the U.S. and the UK. One such group was Debris, formed in Chickasha, Oklahoma, in 1975. Adding synthesizer, organ, saxophone, vibraharp and echo boxes to the mix, Debris created a loopy kind of psychedelic art-punk rock.[39] They played only four live shows in the Oklahoma City area, encountering 'indifference and redneck hostility'. CBGB in New York then offered them a chance to cash in on the punk scene happening there, but by that time Debris had already disbanded.[40]

Other proto-punk bands were lucky enough to take root in active music scenes. Detroit, Michigan, where MC5 and The Stooges ruled the roost, probably had the biggest scene of all. A lesser-known group from the same circles was Up, whose hard-driving sound presaged late British punk and even late 1980s and '90s Sub Pop-style grunge. John Sinclair, the activist who ran the commune where MC5 and Up lived, declared that Up, not MC5 or The Stooges, were the real forefathers of punk.[41] Other notable Detroit-area bands include The Dogs and The Punks, both of whom were known for a thrashing sound that anticipates 1980s hardcore, and Death, a hard-rock band made up of African American brothers whose name alienated many would-be listeners.

New York City had its share of proto-punkers as well, with the New York Dolls at the top of the heap. Often performing alongside the Dolls at the Mercer Arts Center was the anything-but-glam Suicide. Vocalist Alan Vega had been inspired to form Suicide after hearing Silver Apples' electronic music and seeing Iggy Pop put on one of his self-immolating, crowd-baiting performances. The band Vega put together began as a four-piece but evolved into a duo after the guitarist and drummer left, leaving Vega on vocals and Martin Rev on Wurlitzer organ. By 1971, Suicide was already billing itself as 'punk', and the band's early shows took the form of performance art. The two would dress like street thugs, and Vega would shout street poetry over Rev's free-form keyboard noise while swinging a bike chain around his head to threaten the audience. Suicide's confrontational performances, along with their lack of guitar and drums, made them the target of ridicule and violence, and they remained outsiders until they emerged with a set of more conventional songs in 1975; by then, their sound featured throbbing, lo-fi keyboard drones and mechanical beats, over which Vega sang emotionally wrenching lyrics. Their best recordings from this period include a cover of the classic '96 Tears', and 'Ghost Rider', a song named after the Marvel comic book character.

At the other end of the artistic spectrum were The Dictators, a more conventional band that played humorous, hard-edged rock 'n' roll full of sarcastic references to American junk culture. Another technically proficient and innovative New York band was Television, known for playing sinuous, intertwining guitar lines that managed to be highly melodic and rhythmic at the same time. Television also covered several 1960s garage songs, a trait they shared with the Patti Smith Group. This collaboration between Smith and Lenny Kaye – the music critic who gave us *Nuggets* – yielded a mixture of garage rock and spoken-word poetry; fittingly, their first single was a cover of 'Hey Joe' that included a rap about Patty Hearst's experience as a fugitive revolutionary.

Another hotbed for proto-punk groups was Cleveland, Ohio, where bands such as Rocket from the Tombs, The Mirrors and the electric eels played abrasive, angst-filled, pre-punk rock to small audiences. Over in Britain, some parallel proto-punk activity was taking place, with Third World War playing left-wing, revolutionary rock in the MC5 mould, The Hollywood Brats serving as Britain's answer to the New York Dolls, and Cabaret Voltaire conducting sonic experiments with electronic devices and conventional rock instruments.[42] All these bands, whether they knew what they were doing or not, helped to forge the sounds and sensibilities that would soon characterize the 'new music'.

The disparate strands of proto-punk finally coalesced into a movement with a sense of direction and style around 1975 or '76, and observers began referring to this movement as 'New Wave'. During the movement's heady phase of experimentation, before anyone knew quite what to call the music, the terms 'punk' and 'New Wave' were used almost interchangeably, with punk being seen as the new wave that would displace the stodgy mainstream rock of the previous few years. This view pervades a contemporaneous study of punk by Isabelle Anscombe and Dike Blair called *Punk: Punk Rock/ Punk Style/Punk Stance/Punk People/Punk Stars/That Head the New Wave in England and America* (1978). Anscombe, a British scenester, defines punk as an 'attitude of threat' or 'a threatening look which says that the status quo is something that can be changed'.[43] That is, she, like other early participants in the New Wave movement, thought of punk as a form of genuine, individualistic expression that challenged or eroded mainstream culture, in addition to being a style of music.

Accordingly, Anscombe observes that punk expression could take the form of 'music, clothes, style, [or] small magazines called "fanzines"' and adds that 'punk is kids coming together to play rock 'n' roll, edit their papers and get them out onto the streets for other kids to read.'[44] Thus punk had an 'anyone can do it' ethos that involved kids creating their own art to communicate with other kids. Instead of glorifying established stars, the New Wave gave ordinary youngsters the chance to form bands and perform for their peers or to dress up and participate as members of a music scene. Anscombe explains the 'do it yourself' philosophy of punk in this way: 'The kids want to create their own culture and forms of communication, rejecting the star images [as well as] packaged, processed and expensive entertainment . . . The words they listen to are their own, no longer the ideas of some other authority; the performer onstage is one of their mates.'[45] In other words, punks wanted to express themselves, both as performers and spectators, and they wanted to support artists who were their peers instead of older stars who were no longer in touch with the concerns of ordinary youth. In part, this desire reflects the resentment that most youngsters felt about the lifestyles of rich and famous musicians. In Chris Morris's words, 'The rock stars of the day had grown obscenely wealthy and increasingly remote, and behaved almost like imperious royalty', and the 'dole queue' kids of Britain in particular had lost interest in supporting such stars.[46] American youths were less class conscious, but they too found the pampered artists of yesteryear to be out of touch and boring. Given these attitudes, it makes sense that punks would turn back to participatory, dance-oriented rock 'n' roll and away from the passive spectatorship of mainstream corporate rock.

The act of looking back to the past at some 'golden age' of rock 'n' roll for inspiration is one of the qualities of garage rock, and arguably New Wave was the next stage in its development. Just as the 1960s garage musicians turned their backs on the mass-market pop music of their time and looked to the past to find worthwhile material to play as well as authentic modes of expression, New Wave musicians looked back to '60s garage rock and '50s rock 'n' roll to inform their 'back-to-basics' approach. They also strove for vigour, spontaneity and authenticity as opposed to musical virtuosity, and they despised more mainstream music because of its artificiality and calculated commercialism, all of which they associated with musical disingenuousness. However, the amateurism of New Wave was partially feigned, whereas 1960s garage bands were typically made up of local, mostly amateur musicians. It would make sense to call the Ramones or Devo garage bands because they both started as inexperienced neighbourhood guys getting together to make some noise, but it would make no sense to call the Pretenders a garage band because most of their members were seasoned professionals before they joined forces. Likewise, one could justifiably call the Sex Pistols or The Damned garage bands, but not so The Stranglers, most of whom were semi-pro musicians before banding together. Among solo performers, Elvis Costello would be too much of a careerist to be given the 'garage' tag, and Nick Lowe was too much of a professional to qualify: he was a 1960s musician and pub-rocker before riding high on the New Wave. Therefore, even if many New Wave groups were also garage bands, not all were, and New Wave seems to be more of a quasi-garage movement that gave rise to two new genres of rock, namely punk and New Wave. Of course, the terms 'punk' and 'New Wave' have acquired different shades of meaning since 1975/6, with some differences between British and American usage of the terms.

Aficionados of 1960s garage rock were generally sympathetic to and supportive of punk rock; some, like Greg Shaw, were ecstatic about it. Shaw believed that the teenage rock 'n' roll revolution he'd been waiting for all his adult life had finally come to pass. In an editorial called 'In Defense of Rock Theory', originally published in issue 17 of *BOMP!* magazine in November 1977, Shaw writes, 'I believe that something extremely significant is taking place, of which punk rock is only the first symptom, namely the assertion of rock & roll, on its own terms, supported actively and consciously by the people who care about it – us, the fans.'[47] Of course, Shaw also believed that he and his fellow garage-rock enthusiasts were directly responsible for the New Wave revolution, writing further, 'The megalithic world of Led Zep and Elton John is tottering before the slings of a vocal

Greg Shaw first released *Pebbles, Volume 1* to the general public in 1979. Now this series includes nearly 100 albums, and it has been as influential as the *Nuggets* series in spreading the 'garage disease'.

minority who owe their existence to the collective efforts of . . . rock fandom.'[48]

Jumping on the punk bandwagon, Shaw devoted the next four issues of BOMP! to New Wave music, but disillusionment set in quickly. In his editorial for the January 1979 issue, Shaw discusses the 'New Wave recession' brought on by the failure of punk records to capture a mass audience and the weakening of support by the record industry. After some handwringing about the state of American culture and the mindlessness of American consumers, Shaw observes that 'Rock & roll still has the power to break through the crap and ignite our culture, but its attempt to do so through New Wave has failed.'[49] Shaw's downbeat view of the New Wave seems to be based more on his disenchantment with 1970s punk than on actual events, for around the same time he stated in a personal letter to reader Al Quaglieri that he thought BOMP! had taken a wrong turn. He writes: 'You might as well be the first to know. I am planning to change BOMP! back to the kind of magazine it was a few years ago, before punk. I've grown so disenchanted with the current punk scene, it just isn't the fun that '60s rock and collecting fandom used to be.'[50]

In addition to losing interest in 1970s punk, Shaw had also lost interest in publishing fanzines. After 21 issues, BOMP! folded in March 1979 and Shaw put more of his energy into running his two record labels, BOMP! and Voxx. More importantly, however, he found the time in 1978 to begin releasing a new series of '60s garage-rock compilation albums called *Pebbles*. The songs on *Pebbles* were mastered from cassette dubs of the 45s, and Shaw made no attempt to license the songs legally for re-release, but this homemade bootleg series would go on to ignite an even bigger explosion than *Nuggets* in reviving sounds from the past.

5

The Revivalists: Replaying 1960s Garage Rock in the 1980s and Beyond

Following the lead of Greg Shaw, a number of record collectors began issuing their own compilations of obscure 1960s songs in the early 1980s. One such collector was Dave Gibson, who scrounged a record-cutting lathe, formed Moxie Records and produced a ten-volume series of compilation LPS called *Boulders*. Gibson neglected to calibrate his lathe and pulled the singles out of his collection in alphabetical order for mastering, so *Boulders* became notorious for lo-fi sound and haphazard organization.[1] At the opposite end of the spectrum was Tim Warren's *Back from the Grave* series. Boasting hi-fi sound and slang-filled but informative liner notes, BFTG focused entirely on '60s garage punk and entertained record buyers with cover art by Mort Todd, who depicts undead garage rockers torturing characters that represent disco, New Wave, heavy metal and so forth. Some other well-known compilation series from the early 1980s include Shaw's *Pebbles* and *Highs in the Mid-sixties*, *Acid Dreams*, *The Chosen Few*, *Cicadelic '60s*, *Echoes in Time*, *Mindrocker*, *Off the Wall*, *Psychedelic Unknowns*, *Scum of the Earth* and *Texas Punk*. Even though these albums probably had press runs of only 250 to 1,000 copies, at least fifty different titles, including one-off LPS and multi-volume series, hit the marketplace between 1979 and 1985.[2] They showed up in mail-order catalogues and select record stores as far afield as Sweden, helping to spread garage rock to an ever-expanding network of fans.[3]

Tim Warren's *Back from the Grave* series, devoted to '60s garage punk, is the highest quality series of compilation albums on the market, and it now consists of ten LPS (or nine CDS).

These compilations also helped to define the concepts of 'garage rock' and 'garage band' for after-the-fact listeners. Record reviewers began using the 'garage' label in the early 1970s to refer to the kind of local band that practices in someone's home and is made up of aspiring musicians. For instance, Lenny Kaye used the term 'garage band' to make a point in a 1971 review in *Rolling Stone*. Likewise, John Mendelsohn used the term 'punk teenage garage band' in another *Rolling Stone* review the same year. The label stuck because it instantly conveyed an idea of the type of band being referred to, and by the mid-'70s it showed up frequently in reviews published by *Rolling Stone* and *Stereo Review*.[4] Kaye and Greg Shaw mainly used the 'punk' label before using 'garage', but the appropriation of 'punk' by the New Wave movement ended that practice. Some people argue that the 'garage' label is inappropriate because there was no such term in the '60s. Mike Markesich, for example, quotes a period band member, Tom Kirby, who addressed this issue in 2008: 'We always considered ourselves a rock and roll group . . . a teenaged rock & roll combo'.[5] What Kirby says here is valid, but musicians of the 1960s had an insider's view of what they were doing, giving them a limited perspective on the cultural movement of which they were a part. Those of us who are studying that movement from the outside can see a bigger picture from a more objective point of view, and our critical vocabulary shouldn't be restricted by the linguistic or conceptual limitations of the participants themselves. The use of a retroactive term such as 'garage rock' should also serve as a reminder that we are not experiencing the '60s music scene directly; we know it only through representation in various media, some of which include the photos, liner notes and music on compilation albums.

Even before these compilation albums flooded the market, several u.s. bands had already caught the '60s garage bug. The Cramps began serving up their brew of off-kilter rock 'n' roll, rockabilly and garage rock to New York audiences in 1976, mainly opening shows for other bands at Max's Kansas City and CBGB. Boston-based punk band DMZ released an EP in 1977 that included a cover of The 13th Floor Elevators' 'You're Gonna Miss Me'. For their debut LP, DMZ also covered songs by The Sonics, The Wailers and The Troggs. When DMZ broke up in 1978, they reformed as The Lyres, a more '60s-sounding band that released its first single in 1979. Like-minded bands that formed in 1976 include The Fleshtones from Queens, New York, whose first single appeared in 1979, and The Last, a Los Angeles-based power-pop group whose debut album came out on BOMP!, also in 1979. Down in San Diego, The Crawdaddys formed in 1978 and played British-style R&B in the manner of The Pretty Things and The Downliners Sect, releasing their first LP in 1979 and an EP in 1980. The Unclaimed of L.A. formed in 1979 and released an EP on Moxie a year later; their singer's devotion to recreating the '60s sound was so dogged that his first line-up quit on him. However, the most dedicated revival band of all was The Chesterfield Kings, who formed in Rochester, New York, in the late 1970s. The Kings initially swore to play only songs of mid-'60s vintage while using nothing but period musical instruments and wearing only period clothing, and their self-released first single was a cover of The Brogues' 'I Ain't No Miracle Worker' backed by

The Cramps' repertoire included '60s garage classics such as Randy Alvey and the Green Fuz's 'Green Fuz' and Count Five's 'Psychotic Reaction'.

Promo photo of DMZ, a '70s punk band that covered a number of '60s garage-rock songs and helped to usher in the garage revival of the 1980s. After breaking up in 1978, DMZ reformed as The Lyres, a neo-garage band.

The Heard's 'Exit 9'.[6] Obviously, the idea of mining the 1960s for material to play was floating around in the '70s, but revival bands were too few and far between to constitute much of a movement.

That situation changed when Shaw decided to form Voxx, a label dedicated to releasing 1960s revival music. At first, Shaw had trouble finding enough authentic-sounding material, so he organized a 'Battle of the Bands' like the ones of yore, except that the bands' songs would appear on an album and record buyers would vote for the best song. The scheme worked well enough for Shaw to release the first volume of *Battle of the Garages* in 1981.[7] Even though BOTG was the first-ever compilation of '80s neo-garage music, most of the tracks on the LP sound more like warmed-over New Wave or power pop than '60s garage music; fortunately, cover songs by The Mystic Eyes, The Slickee Boys and The Chesterfield Kings redeem the whole project. Shaw then organized an East Coast tour for groups on the LP, and bands such as The Hypsterz, Vertebrats, Plasticland, The Slickee Boys and The Wombats played in every major city from Minneapolis to New York.[8] The musicians sported 1960s clothing and pageboy haircuts while deploying Vox and Rickenbacker guitars and Farfisa organs, and a movement was kicked off, fuelled by the proliferation of '60s compilation albums and neo-garage bands.[9] From this time forward, garage rock flowed in two different but intermingled streams, and listeners would have to think about whether they were hearing music recorded in the 1960s or the '80s, and whether the songs were originals or covers.

Young people of the 1980s were drawn to the '60s garage-rock revival for several reasons, some of which were caused by the waning of the New Wave movement. As punk ossified into hardcore, many club patrons were turned off by its emphasis on testosterone-fuelled aggression instead of creative rebellion. Simultaneously, New Wave had given rise to synth-pop and electronic dance music, yet many club-goers still wanted to hear guitar-driven rock 'n' roll that was more danceable and lighthearted than punk; for them, neo-garage music seemed to hit the spot. In addition to the sounds, the '60s revival offered a look that was recognizable and yet alternative enough to be 'underground'.[10] Guys could wear striped T-shirts, black turtlenecks or paisley shirts along with black stovepipe trousers and Beatle boots, while girls could wear dresses with

THE SONICS '66

THE SONICS '80

Contact: Paul Grant, BOMP Records. P.O. Box 7112, Burbank, CA 91510 (213) 227-4141

Promo photo of a short-lived reincarnation of The Sonics that consisted of vocalist Jerry Roslie and rock band The Invaders. In 1980, Roslie and his crew cut an album called *Sinderella* for BOMP! Records; the LP included several covers of Sonics tunes, but they lacked the power and charm of the originals.

pop-art prints or miniskirts and go-go boots, expressing their hip sensibilities while also distinguishing themselves from regular patrons of '80s nightclubs. Moreover, the '60s revival offered the same kind of audience participation that made New Wave so appealing in the beginning; scenesters could dress up and hang out with like-minded individuals in the clubs, watching musician friends of theirs play onstage. Rich Coffee, guitarist and vocalist for Thee Fourgiven, recalls the togetherness of the LA scene: 'I always think of the parties, the friends, the incredible supporters of the scene, the solidarity and especially the FUN that we all had together.'[11] Coffee's observation about the tight-knit community of the '60s revival scene in LA raises another point: the idea that participating in this scene was a great deal of fun for everyone involved.

By the early 1980s, every city in America probably had at least one band that played some '60s garage songs, but the two main scenes existed in Los Angeles and New York. The leading light of the LA scene was Greg Shaw, of course, and in 1985 he opened a venue on Hollywood Boulevard called The Cavern Club. A small, dingy room with a crappy sound system, The Cavern Club became *the* place to play for neo-garage/neo-psych bands, although nightclubs such as Raji's, Club Lingerie, Music Machine, Anti-Club and The Shamrock also hosted neo-garage shows.[12] The Cavern also served as home for the 'Paisley Underground', Michael Quercio's name for a circle of bands that included Green on Red, The Bangles, The Dream Syndicate and Quercio's own The Three O'Clock.[13] As the hip place to be, The Cavern Club had a dress code, and visitors who showed up in attire other than that of 1960s vintage were made to feel unwelcome.[14] Subsequently, music journalists who visited the Cavern wondered if the revival was more about fashion or music. For instance, Greg Turner asked in a March 1986 article for *Creem* whether the neo-garage movement was a 'passing fad or mounting groundswell? Fashion show or swap meet?'[15] In an article for BAM magazine in June 1986, Frank Beeson described The Cavern Club as 'a gathering of Neanderthal hairstyles, turtlenecks, paisley, and Carnaby Street fashions'.[16] Naturally, musicians took exception to this reductive view and argued that the music was paramount. Thee Fourgiven's Coffee observed that '[The fashion] is not the main thing going on here. It's the music that is so important, and nobody is paying attention to that.'[17] While it is true that most journalists tended to gloss over the music and latched on to the visual style of the movement, many of the scene's regulars focused more on fashion themselves. Local scene member Frank Mamlin comments, 'Fashion goes hand in hand with the music. I mean, this is Hollywood! That's what we came here for!'[18] Obviously, 1960s revivalists in LA valued one aspect of the movement or another based on their own personal roles in the scene.

New York bands tended to play fuzz-laden garage punk with snotty vocals as opposed to the subdued neo-psych and jangly pop-psych favoured by their counterparts in LA. The New York scene revolved around The Dive, a cabaret that, in fairness, was less of a dive than The Cavern Club. The space had the ambience of a Vincent Price movie, with burning torches and skeletons hanging from chains on both sides of the stage. In 1982, a neo-garage act called The Cheepskates became the house band,[19] but The Dive also hosted such '60s revival bands as The Outta Place, The Tryfles, The Fuzztones, The Vipers, Mad Violets and Mod Fun. By the mid-1980s The Dive had become the cool place to play, with bands such as The Headless Horsemen, The Optic Nerve, The Raunch Hands and The Secret Service performing there.[20] Yet New York was not a one-venue town; these bands could also play Irving Plaza and the Peppermint Lounge.

The mover and shaker behind the New York scene was J. D. Martignon, a French record dealer who created the first record label in New York for neo-garage music. Martignon got his start by selling French reissues of 1950s R&B and rockabilly to Venus Records in the East Village. After putting ads in *Goldmine* magazine to sell his French imports, he began obtaining 1960s garage compilations and selling them from his apartment to local music fans. Business snowballed, so he opened Midnight Records, a record store and label, in 1984.[21] His label issued neo-garage/neo-psych, rockabilly and underground pop records, and the first release was an LP by

The Zantees, whose members included the founders of Norton Records, Billy Miller and Miriam Linna.[22] Martignon went on to issue records by Plan 9, The Outta Place, The Tryfles, The Fuzztones and The Cheepskates.[23] Artists received only small advances for their recordings and no royalties, so he developed a reputation as a shady hustler whose accounting practices were murky at best.[24] Nevertheless, bands on Midnight did receive national and international distribution of their records, and Martignon's mail-order catalogue, *The Midnight Tymes*, helped to propagate garage-revival music around the globe.[25] For example, record stores in Italy had sections just for Midnight Records, and discs by The Outta Place and Plan 9 were No. 1 and 2 in the Italian indie charts in the mid-1980s.[26] However, things went downhill for Midnight in the early 1990s as rock fanzines disappeared and the label lost its best avenue for advertising. In addition, some artists contend that Midnight lacked the staff and resources to promote its product, and Dave Herrera, guitarist and vocalist for The Cheepskates, explains that as tastes in the rock world changed, Martignon put out records by mediocre bands with awful cover art, and so the label lost money before coming to an end in 1993.[27] In spite of his failings, Martignon did give garage-revival bands of the 1980s a way to document their musical efforts and to make a splash beyond the New York scene.

One of the best compilation albums documenting the West and East Coast scenes is *Garage Sale: 19 Wyld and Savage Bands!*, a cassette tape-only release sponsored by *Goldmine* magazine and issued by ROIR Cassettes in 1985. Fanzines of the 1980s often issued homemade cassette tapes, but *Garage Sale* was professionally produced. The cover art, drawn by The Fuzztones' Rudi 'Action' Protrudi, depicts a 'caveman' playing a Vox guitar while wearing a turtleneck, Maltese cross, furry vest, skintight paisley pants and Beatle boots. This 'cave people' trope expresses the idea that garage rockers were wild and primitive brutes who wielded Vox guitars instead of clubs, and it commonly appeared in 1980s neo-garage art.

Garage Sale has some outstanding cover songs on it, including The Fuzztones' rendition of 'Cinderella', The Shoutless' version of 'I Tell No Lies' and The Vipers' cover of 'Who Dat?' The hottest originals include The Gravedigger Five's snotty garage-punk 'She Got', Boys from Nowhere's catchy 'Beg' and The Pandoras' punk anthem 'Hot Generation'. Other well-known acts appearing on *Garage Sale* include The Mosquitos, The Trip, Mystic Eyes, The Tell-tale Hearts, Thee Fourgiven, The Cheepskates and The Unclaimed. *Garage Sale* comes close to capturing the energy and sound of 1960s garage, although the album contains very little neo-psych; it would have been more well-rounded had it included selections by The Rain Parade, Mad Violets, Plan 9 or Plasticland, but a compilation album has to leave something out.

Photo of *Garage Sale*, one of the best compilations of American garage-revival music of the 1980s. The cassette tape's cover art by Rudi 'Action' Protrudi, featuring a hip 'caveman', shows how garage revivalists imagined the primitive rockers of the 1960s.

Across the Atlantic in Britain, the garage revival was less straightforward. Many bands played '60s garage rock blended with other styles of music, and a few played them in the guise of 'trash rock', a crude form of rock 'n' roll that, at its rawest, exhibits unpolished, gravelly singing, abrasive guitar textures laced with feedback, unbalanced harmonic content (for example too much treble and too little bass) and sloppy starts and finishes. The leading exponent of trash rock was Mike Spenser, a Brooklynite who emigrated to London in 1975 and sang with several hard R&B/pub-rock bands before forming The Cannibals. They covered dozens of '60s garage songs, putting out at least ten LPS as well as EPS and singles.[28] Spenser worked continuously to push garage rock and create a scene in London; for one thing, he convinced nightclubs to host his 'Nights of Trash' events, pulling bands such as The Sting-Rays and Mickey and the Milkshakes into his trash-rock fold.[29] Early on, The Sting-Rays played Cramps-style trashabilly, but they later concocted a blend of rockabilly, American roots music, power pop and 1960s garage rock. The Milkshakes, one of Billy Childish's many bands, was a rhythm-and-beat combo that put out ten or so LPS, one of which was fittingly called *Thee Knights of Trash* (1984). A typical Milkshakes' song is 'Please Don't Tell My Baby', an urgent R&B number with a Duane Eddy-style guitar riff and raspy male vocals. To promote garage-related music of this kind, Spenser formed his own label, HIT Records, and issued several compilation albums.[30]

The scene cultivated by Spenser did draw in some bands that had nothing to do with trash rock. These bands, including The Prisoners, The Playn Jayn, The Barracudas and The Dentists,[31] all sounded different from one another, but the common thread tying them together was 1960s-flavoured power pop. The most successful of this lot were The Barracudas, who began by reviving vocal surf music. In early singles such as 'I Want My Woody Back', 'Summer Fun' and '(I Wish It Could Be) 1965 Again', The 'Cudas combine Beach Boys-style vocal harmonies with the melodic punk sound of the Buzzcocks. Given that these songs were recorded in 1979 and 1980, it makes sense that they would have the dynamics and power-chord texture of New Wave. However, their lyrics and spoken-word sections express nostalgia for mid-'60s American youth culture, particularly in '1965 Again', which ends with references to 'Hey Joe', 'Louie Louie', *Shindig!*, *Hullabaloo*, *Surf City* and so on. The B-side of their first LP, *Drop Out with The Barracudas* (1981), is saturated with these nostalgic looks at the past, while the A-side features songs that blend '60s folk-rock, garage and psych with wistful power pop.[32] The infectious sound of The Barracudas' songs reminded people just how delightful '60s pop could be and helped to trigger a surf revival in London; The Surfin' Lungs emerged in 1981, sounding very similar to The 'Cudas, while The Surfadelics, despite their name, shunned Beach Boys-style harmonies and sounded more like a true '60s garage combo.

The Barracudas were part of London's psychedelic revival, but the first band to delve into psychedelia was The Soft Boys, a late '70s group that was out of step with their New Wave contemporaries; they looked up to Pink Floyd's Syd Barrett and played trippy power pop with quirky rhythms, incongruent parts and surrealistic lyrics but also strong melodies and dual guitar lines like those of Television. After putting out an EP in 1977, The Soft Boys followed up with an LP, *A Can of Bees* (1979), which gets closer to New Wave but also has some Captain Beefheart-like moments. Their second LP, *Underwater Moonlight* (1980), has a more commercial sound, displaying catchy melodies and the chiming folk-guitar sound of The Byrds and Fairport Convention.[33] Music of this sort sparked an urge to revive the discotheques, cellar nightclubs and Carnaby Street fashions of Swinging London; several events in 1981 also gave momentum to the psychedelic reawakening, one of which was the paperback edition of *No One Here Gets Out Alive*, the best-selling biography of Jim Morrison by Jerry Hopkins and Danny Sugerman. Another was the release of *Altered States*, a Ken Russell film, which rejuvenated interest in the mind-altering possibilities of hallucinogens. Finally, the Grateful Dead played a series of shows at London's Rainbow, giving young Britons a glimpse of the turned-on '60s.[34]

The psych revival in London was under way by the spring of 1981. Neo-psych bands performed in venues such as The Groovy Cellar, The Clinic and Le Kilt in Soho;[35] other venues included Merlin's Cave, The Garage, 100 Club and Alice in Wonderland, which was the epicentre of the UK neo-psych scene for a while.[36] Club patrons bought their '60s outfits at The Regal or Sweet Charity in Kensington Market, where they could find the 'paisley shirts, kaftans, chiffon blouses, and kinky boots' they needed to make the scene in style.[37] The best musical document of this neo-psych scene is the compilation *A Splash of Colour* (1981), featuring songs by Mood Six, Miles Over Matter, The Times, The Earwigs, The Marble Staircase and The Silence, among others. The strongest tracks on the LP are by The High Tide; 'Dancing in My Mind' features prominent bass lines, guitar arpeggios, spacey, high-pitched sounds, clear male vocals and haunting female chorus parts, while 'Electric Blue' starts with a 'Morning Dew' feel and builds to an energetic jam with driving bass lines and keyboards. Otherwise, *A Splash of Colour* consists of melancholy flower-power pop that seems pretty tame by '60s standards.

Comparable scenes – albeit much smaller ones – sprang up around the world. The European countries of France, Spain, Germany, Italy, Sweden, Greece and the Netherlands became especially strong markets for garage revival music. Many countries even had radio shows devoted to garage music, including *Electric Fit* (Italy) and *Fuzz Box* (Spain). In North America, Canada had *The Fuzz that Wuzz* and *Garage Grooves* with Amazing Larry, and the U.S. had *Acid Rain* and Rodney Bingenheimer's KROQ show.[38] Fanzines like *Who Put the Bomp* had also sprung up to spread the word: France had *Nineteen*, Germany had *Splendid* and *hartbeat!*, Sweden had *Larm* and the UK had *Next Big Thing*, *Communication Blur* and *Bucketful of*

Brains.[39] Some of the best revival bands from international scenes include The Cryptones (France), Sex Museum and Los Negativos (Spain), The Broken Jug and Shiny Gnomes (Germany), The Sick Rose and Technicolor Dreams (Italy), The Sound Explosion (Greece), The Other Side and The Kliek (the Netherlands), Cosmic Dropouts and The Lust-O-Rama (Norway) and The Creeps, The Stomach-mouths, Watermelon Men, Wylde Mammoths and The Nomads (Sweden). Beyond Europe were The Ten Commandments and The Worst (Canada), The Chills (New Zealand) and The Bo-Weevils, the Hoodoo Gurus and Lime Spiders (Australia). Out of the many '80s garage-revival bands across the world, the greatest is probably Sweden's Nomads; not only did they play hard-rocking yet atmospheric garage music, both covers and originals, but they did some of the most moving and satisfying interpretations of American roots rock ever recorded.[40]

That being said, very little garage-revival music measures up to the original songs of the '60s. In general, neo-garage music pleases the ear and moves the body, but it lacks the verve of the original scene. The difference is clear if one compare's The Chocolate Watch-band's 'Are You Gonna Be There? (At the Love-in)' or The Shades of Night's 'Fluctuation' with The Chesterfield Kings' covers of those songs. The Kings' versions are well done but not quite as intense or as wild. Even the best originals from the '80s lack something heard in the best '60s songs. Randy Alvey and the Green Fuz's 'Green Fuz' is a crude, barely audible piece of teenage braggadocio, but it has a pathos and strangeness unmatched by any garage song from the '80s. The disparities are no fault of these later musicians, who lived in different social and cultural milieus from the original creators of garage rock. The 1960s were a time of sunshine and blue skies, with a feeling in the air that anything was possible, whereas the 1980s were a time of navy-blue suits and concrete-and-glass enclosures, and a malaise filled the air – no wonder a '60s revival occurred in the '80s.

Young garage musicians of the 1960s were fortunate enough to live during a time of explosive change and creativity. The parameters of rock music were still being explored and defined, so '60s musicians had more freedom to fool around and figure out what sounded good, whereas '80s musicians inherited a more rigidly defined and codified genre of music that would quickly turn into something other than garage rock if they experimented with it too much. Moreover, teenage garage rockers of the 1960s played with 'beginner's mind': they could play in a fresher, more original way because of their own lack of expertise, while '80s revivalist musicians were too knowledgeable and therefore too constrained by ideas about what was 'good' or 'bad', or what was 'acceptable', 'cool' or 'authentic', to play freely. Being less studied, '60s garage musicians could create ear-opening sonic textures – no matter how raunchy or bizarre – that would have been heard as unacceptable by more experienced musicians, enabling '60s teen rockers to create primal music that moves the listener viscerally in addition to cerebrally.

In spite of the greater appeal of '60s music, we should appreciate the '80s revivalists for putting so much energy and passion into playing garage and psychedelic rock; they made life in the decade much more interesting and tolerable. Many young people then were yuppies who believed that happiness lay in consuming material goods; by contrast, the garage revivalists were bohemians who lived by humanistic values and for artistic expression, and their revival of '60s youth culture remained an underground movement with little chance of gaining mass acceptance. Indeed, '80s garage bands had little hope of shoving the Duran Durans or Depeche Modes aside in the marketplace and having their retro sounds receive airplay on commercial radio or having their videos played on MTV. Yet the garage revivalists did help to create an atmosphere in which it was cool for more commercially viable groups to adopt the sounds and fashions of the 1960s; some major-label groups that exploited this 'back to the past' impulse include The B-52's, The Jesus and Mary Chain, the Pretenders and Echo and the Bunnymen.[41]

Even if 1980s garage bands had little hope of enjoying the same success as the behemoths of alternative rock, they played on, touring and churning out vinyl discs and cassette tapes. Understandably,

Ugly Things has been devoted to memorializing forgotten rock 'n' roll bands since 1983. Founder Mike Stax himself played bass guitar for The Crawdaddys, a San Diego revivalist band in the mould of The Pretty Things and Downliners Sect.

most bands grew tired of adhering to the '60s formula after a while and their music evolved into hybrid forms of underground rock, but the groups that moved on were always replaced by others that were still devoted to the garage sound. Timothy Gassen observes that the '80s neo-garage movement flowed in waves with two-year cycles, each wave being renewed by an influx of new bands and scene members after petering out. When the garage revival apparently died out in the u.s. around 1990, a new wave of neo-garage and neo-psych bands swelled up in Europe during 1992 and kept the revival going.[42] Amazingly, the garage revival lasted a good fifteen years or more, while the original mid-'60s garage period had only lasted about four, clearly demonstrating that garage rock filled a need that was not being met by the mainstream popular music of the 1980s and '90s.

Fortunately for garage-ophiles, the stream of albums compiling obscure 1960s songs continued to flow throughout the '80s and '90s. Enthusiasts kept on discovering worthwhile recordings by '60s garage combos, something that surprised even a few record collectors. Record buyers, however, had become more discriminating by the '90s and expected well-produced compilation albums instead of the cruddy bootlegs of old. Tim Warren's *Back from the Grave* (2010–15) and *Last of the Garage Punk Unknowns* (2010–16) series on Crypt Records had set the standards for high-quality sound, liner notes, photos and packaging, and many record companies followed suit.[43] Cicadelic released several excellent compilation series on CD during the 1990s, including the eight-volume *Cicadelic 60s*, the five-volume *History of Texas Garage Bands* and the one-shot *The Heart Beats and Other Texas Girls of the '60s*. Collectables released the three-volume *Acid Visions* and ten-volume *Green Crystal Ties*, both of which added many psych songs to the garage canon. Some other notable compilation series include Eva Records' eight-volume *Sixties Archive* and Romulan's *Girls in the Garage*, also eight volumes. Two other series that made a stir during the 1990s are the fifteen-volume *Teenage*

Shutdown and Hans Kesteloo's sixteen-volume *Sixties Rebellion*, which features humorous artwork by none other than Rudi 'Action' Protrudi. While none of these series can match the consistently good garage-punk selections found on *Back from the Grave*, they do offer a wider variety of tracks done in other styles. This ever-expanding archive of '60s garage songs, along with the body of music created during the garage revival, resulted in a new musical realm that would have been astounding to someone like Lester Bangs, who died in 1982 and whose exposure to '60s groups was pretty much limited to the ones featured on *Nuggets* and *Pebbles*. If he had lived to see the twenty-first century, Bangs would have seen this ballooning body of garage music usher in yet another series of garage-related genres during the 2000s.

6

The Backtrackers: Garage Rock in the Twenty-first Century

While the garage revival was sputtering out in the U.S. in the late 1980s, a new style of garage-related rock emerged. Called 'garage punk', this new variation on old genres bears some relation to 1960s garage punk, but it stands apart from '80s garage-revival rock because it has little interest in slavishly imitating the sounds or fashions of the 1960s.[1] With regard to image and presentation, garage punks often wear bizarre, theatrical get-ups when performing. The Mummies, one of the first garage-punk bands, wear just what one would expect – head-to-ankle mummy suits made of white rags. Contemporary garage-punk artist King Khan will sometimes wear hot pants and a gold lamé cape onstage, while Nobunny will appear in dirty white briefs and a bunny mask pulled from a stuffed toy animal.[2] Outlandish appearances aside, garage punks play with the energy and abrasiveness of 1970s punk, often striving to make the same kind of rhythmic noise made by Detroit proto-punk groups such as Up, MC5 and The Stooges.[3] Yet garage punks play material derived from blues, R&B, surf rock, 1960s girl-group pop, garage rock, power pop and hard-core punk, causing Beverly Bryan to define garage punk as a genre 'inspired by all the ragged roots of rock 'n' roll . . . including all earlier incarnations of punk itself'.[4] Thus garage punks are like all other garage rockers in the sense that they look back at previous forms of music in their search for inspiration and authenticity.

Despite looking to the past, this form of rock is not revivalist in nature. As King Khan observes, 'I don't think of it as revivalism. I think of it as carrying on a tradition of rock 'n' roll, without being purist.'[5] As we have already seen, this distinction helps to define garage rock in general: it tries to capture the energy and spirit of earlier genres of rock 'n' roll without being too hung up on accurately recreating the past. Eric Friedl, who has been a member of garage-punk bands The Oblivians and The Reatards, reinforces this idea when he states, 'This kind of rock isn't really revivalist in nature . . . It's a case of songwriters going through the archives and seeing where others left some unfinished business in their haste to embrace the future.'[6]

Friedl's point here is well made; musical trends come and go way too quickly for musicians to exhaust all the possibilities of every style that comes along, but garage punk gives musicians the opportunity to go back and play songs by Chuck Berry or Eddie Cochran in a new way. In discovering artists from the past, garage punks may also find that forgotten performers had the same interests and values they have. For instance, a garage punk may discover that The Sonics were blasting out deranged rock 'n' roll way back in mid-1960s Seattle, and then find out that The Sonics were themselves channelling Little Richard, an eccentric performer who wore make-up and shouted out rock 'n' roll while living a bisexual lifestyle. Most garage punks have found out about ignored, forgotten music from the past by listening to the compilation albums issued by Crypt and Norton records, causing Eric Davidson, music journalist and frontman for New Bomb Turks, to suggest that the roots of garage punk are to be found in these compilations.[7]

These albums also gave garage punks a template to follow for 'punkifying' songs from the past. A case in point is The Gories, one of the founding bands in the garage-punk movement and one of Detroit's finest. The band started in the mid-1980s as three friends who loved records and '60s culture; a couple of them even fancied themselves latter-day Mods and thus listened to the blues and R&B music that influenced the British Invasion bands.[8] They also listened to the *Back from the Grave* compilations, amazed that these teenaged cats in the mid-1960s could play such raw, primal covers of Chess blues songs, and the soon-to-be Gories figured that if teenagers back than could do that, they could too.[9] With no prior experience on their instruments, Mick Collins and Dan Kroha both took up guitar and Peggy O'Neill took up the drums. As The Gories, they began thrashing out primitive rhythm and blues. By necessity, they had a stripped-down aesthetic; they had no bass because someone had to play rhythm guitar and someone had to play lead,[10] and O'Neill bought an old drum set with no head on the kick drum and no cymbals or hi-hat, so she pounded out the beat on three tom-toms. The Gories' live shows were drunken shambles, but guitarist Kroha points out that even though they were technically 'bad' musicians, they had the balls to get out and perform while being that bad.[11] The band managed to record three outstanding LPs in between break-ups, creating such classic songs as 'Feral', 'Thunderbird ESQ', and 'Hey, Hey, We're the Gories'. The band still performs one-off shows today and is considered to be one of the founders of 'punk blues'[12] – even though '60s bands such as New York's Groupies, Australia's Missing Links and the Netherlands' Q65 were playing punk blues some twenty years earlier!

Another early garage-punk band that displays its knowledge of 1960s music while creating garage-rock mayhem is The Mummies. The rag-wrapped foursome play dumb in interviews, but they obviously know '60s garage rock. In 1990 they released a single that covers two songs by The Wailers, and the cover art is a parody of the classic photo of The Wailers taken while 'Tall Cool One' was a hit. They have also Mummified several classic garage songs, including The Sonics' 'Shot Down' as well as two Texas garage gems: The Six Pents' 'She Lied' and Larry and the Bluenotes' 'In and Out'. The self-styled 'kings of budget rock' play vintage instruments salvaged

On the cover of their *Never Been Caught* LP, the 'kings of budget rock' pose with their Mummy-mobile.

from pawn shops and thrift stores; in fact, one of their first singles was recorded in a thrift store in Redwood City, California, where they had scored a Farfisa organ, Silvertone amp and hot-rod sound-effect record just weeks before.[13] They travel to gigs in their vintage Pontiac Bonneville station wagon/ambulance and play in a frantic, loose style, with the organist/vocalist falling down and climbing all over his keyboard. The Mummies often seem to be playing down to the worst of their abilities, with the guitarist playing clunky riffs on well-known songs to keep from sounding too slick, yet their own original songs are pretty infectious even if the sound is lo-fi and monaural. Like The Gories, The Mummies have broken up and re-formed many times, but they continue to make appearances at one-off shows and festivals such as Ponderosa Stomp (in 2017) and Burger Boogaloo (in 2015 and 2016).

Mass popularity eludes bands like The Gories and The Mummies, but garage punk lives on as a thriving underground movement to this day. Demonstrating once again that garage rock is the avant-garde of rock music, garage punk has paved the way for the success of more mainstream garage-rock acts, including The Strokes, The Hives, The Vines and The White Stripes. These are the Big Four of post-millennium garage rock, the ones that music journalists praised in the early 2000s for creating the first commercially successful garage rock.[14] The White Stripes were even hailed by *Spin* and *Rolling Stone* as 'the saviors of rock and roll'.[15] Out of this lot, The Stripes

The Hives, of Fagersta, Sweden, rose to mainstream prominence after the release of *Veni Vidi Vicious* (2000), their second album.

As a duo, The White Stripes boiled rock down to its essentials: guitar, drums and vocals.

are the least conventional, being a two-piece band without a bass player. Founder Jack White grew up in the Detroit music scene and absorbed the minimalism he saw there. He readily acknowledges his debt to The Gories, from whom he learned that a 'primitive' and 'simple' approach to rock could work.[16] He obviously borrowed the idea of having an inexperienced girl play the drums from The Gories, putting his then wife Meg White on the skins. Early on, locals found Meg's inept drumming to be charming, and when someone commented that she looked like a little kid playing the drums, Jack was pleased.[17] He told an interviewer that the band was a way to get back to childhood without being a comedy act.[18]

However, Jack developed more of a conceptual, studied minimalism than his Detroit peers, using concepts taken from the De Stijl art movement of the 1920s to create the artwork for their albums as well as the colour scheme for their own clothing – they dressed only in red, white and black.[19] They even went so far as to title their second album *De Stijl* (2000). On this and their first album, The White Stripes play three kinds of material, the first being Led Zeppelinesque tunes stripped down to monster guitar riffs and booming drums, accompanied by Jack's Robert Plant-like vocals. The second, covers of blues songs such as Son House's 'Death Letter' and Blind Willie McTell's 'Your Southern Can is Mine', feature Jack playing slide guitar and singing in a straightforward, respectful style – no garage punk here. In the third, Jack plays mournful, minor-key songs that sound pretty nondescript next to the whang and thump of the Zeppelin-flavoured rockers. What qualifies The White Stripes' music as 'garage' is its honest, homemade quality; both the guitars and the drums have an upfront presence in the mix, sounding like real instruments played by human beings.

Other bands making a noise during the post-millennium garage/psych resurgence include a number of groups from the Detroit scene such as The Von Bondies, The Hentchmen, The Dirtbombs and The Detroit Cobras. Down south in Memphis, Tennessee, garage-punk trio Oblivians took after The Gories by playing with no bass guitar or bass drum. Over in Chatham, England, the ever-prolific Billy Childish kept churning out infectious garage rock 'n' roll with Thee Headcoats and The Buff Medways. In Umeå, Sweden, The (International) Noise Conspiracy played punk/garage rock while singing lyrics that espoused a left-wing political agenda. Further east in Tokyo, Japan, a female trio called The 5.6.7.8's blended American surf, rockabilly and garage rock to create a sound so engaging that Quentin Tarantino hired them to perform a few songs in *Kill Bill: Volume 1* (2003).

Another wave of bands that enjoyed various degrees of international success by playing garage-related rock include New Zealand's The D4, Australia's Jet and the UK's Arctic Monkeys and The

Libertines. In the U.S., several underground bands rose to various levels of mainstream popularity as their songwriting matured and they developed a more multidimensional approach to garage rock. The Black Lips, a garage-punk outfit from Atlanta, were known mainly for slinging vomit, urine, saliva and blood around during their early shows. They also played with a juvenile punk attitude, creating 1970s-style punk with distorted vocals along with trashed-out, lo-fi blues. As the years passed and they became more proficient on their instruments, their songs became more accessible, and by 2006 the *New York Times* and *Rolling Stone* were singing their praises.[20] As of 2017, The Black Lips' profile has risen high enough that their latest album, *Satan's Graffiti or God's Art?*, was produced by Sean Lennon.[21] Another fixture in twenty-first-century garage rock is Thee Oh Sees, a San Francisco-based group that started off as a solo recording project by John Dwyer called OCS and evolved into a band that became known for its high-energy live shows and prodigious recorded output. Sounding early on like a lo-fi take on The Mamas and the Papas, Thee Oh Sees' sound has since veered back and forth between gritty garage/punk rock and melodic psych-pop.[22]

A garage rocker with ties to Thee Oh Sees is Ty Segall, who has worked on side projects with Dwyer. Segall has been thrashing out lo-fi garage rock as a solo artist since 2008. Influenced by rock acts ranging from David Bowie, Marc Bolan, Black Sabbath and Hawkwind to The Beatles, The Byrds, the Grateful Dead and Neil Young, Segall's songwriting has become so eclectic that he transcends genre; his latest album, *Ty Segall* (2017), hops around from one style to another and contains elements of hardcore punk, Dylan-esque country rock, Grateful Dead jams, piano-based pop and Sabbath riffs.[23] Another garage-rock act that has found mainstream success by escaping the constraints of genre is The Black Keys, a blues-rock duo like The White Stripes that strips rock music down to the essential guitar and drums. After establishing themselves and jumping to a major record label in 2006, The Keys began to stray from their raw garage-blues sound. In 2008 the duo worked with the hip-hop artist and producer Danger Mouse, to record *Attack & Release*. Then the band recorded a rap/rock album called *Blakroc* (2009). After a return to blues on *Brothers* (2010), The Keys recorded *El Camino* (2011), a rock 'n' roll album that went to No. 2 in the Billboard charts; they followed this with a psychedelic album called *Turn Blue* (2014), which went to No. 1 in the U.S., Canada and Australia.[24] Without a doubt, The Keys are the most popular garage-related rock act today.

Before this garage/psych resurgence, another phenomenon that began taking place in the 1980s and continues today is the reunion of defunct rock bands; seemingly every rock group from the famous to the completely unknown has reunited to have another go at it, including many garage combos from the '60s. One such act is The Sloths, a Los Angeles-based band that began at Beverly Hills High in 1964.[25] The band is known mainly by garage-rock fanatics for 'Makin' Love', a song with a Bo Diddley beat and a lurching riff that goes buh-dump, duh-DUMP. Even though the lyrics were too racy for radio, the song was so catchy that a couple of other '60s bands covered it. In 2011, Mike Stax of the *Ugly Things* fanzine published an interview with a surviving Sloth, who then linked up with another ex-member and reunited the band. The Sloths then began performing in LA nightclubs in 2012, reliving their mid-'60s heyday when they played Pandora's Box and The Sea Witch on the Sunset Strip, and the kids who see The Sloths perform today still consider them 'badass'.[26] Moreover, after some recent line-up changes, The Sloths have released a new album called *Back from the Grave* (2015), an unoriginal but appropriate title fifty years after their release of 'Makin' Love'.

Another reunited garage band from California is The Chocolate Watchband. More accomplished than The Sloths, The Watchband gigged around the Bay Area in the 1960s, playing Stones-flavoured R&B with a ferocious punk intensity. The band released three LPS, two EPS and four singles during its time together and performed in teensploitation movies such as *Riot on Sunset Strip* (1967) and *The Love-ins* (1967). However, the members considered themselves primarily a live act that, in the words of vocalist Dave Aguilar, 'loved to challenge big-name acts and blow them off the stage'.[27] After being undermined by manager/producer Ed Cobb, several key members quit the band in 1968. Aguilar became a professor of astronomy and later worked in the aerospace industry.[28] In the meantime, The Watchband's reputation grew as its songs appeared on a dozen or more compilation albums, and the band developed a cult following after being defunct for roughly two decades.[29] Exploring the possibility of reuniting in the mid-1990s, Aguilar and a couple of ex-members found substitutes to fill in for two other original members, and the band re-formed to play shows at the '66-99' event in San Diego and Cavestomp '99 in New York, sharing the bill with fellow '60s groups The Standells and The Monks.[30] Still active as of 2015, The Watchband has performed at festivals throughout the U.S. and Europe, and fans report that they still put on a fiery show.[31] They have also recorded and released a couple of new albums, one being a concert album called *At the Love-in Live!* (2001) from their Cavestomp appearance.[32]

When The Monks headlined at Cavestomp '99, they were not only playing together for the first time in 32 years, they were playing their first-ever gig in America.[33] After the band broke up in Germany in 1967, the members returned to the States and went their separate ways. During the 1990s, bassist Eddie Shaw became aware that The Monks had a passionate following among fans of garage rock, so he contacted other members of the group, leading to a reunion of the original line-up.[34] Their performance at Cavestomp was ecstatically received, and a review in the *New York Times* states that The Monks were 'untouched by time or fashion' as they 'tore into' their well-known songs from *Black Monk Time* (1966).[35] The band performed again in 2004 at the Rockaround event in Las Vegas;

Cavestomp is a garage-rock festival held periodically in New York City. Founding sponsor Jon Weiss was a member of The Vipers, who held their own 'cavestomp' shows back in the 1980s.

but mortality intervened when drummer Roger Johnston died of cancer later that year. In 2006 a documentary called *The Monks: The Transatlantic Feedback* premiered in Chicago, and the band appeared in London, Zurich and Berlin. When banjo player Dave Day died in 2008, The Monks retired again.[36] However, as of 2011 Shaw was still recording jazz, funk, dada rock and 'pissed-off' pop, while frontman Gary Burger played solo shows that included songs by The Monks until he passed away in 2014 after battling cancer.[37] Many Monks fans were dismayed but thankful that they had at least had an opportunity to experience such a legendary band.

Another great '60s group that has had a good run in the twenty-first century is The Sonics, who were asked by Jon Weiss of Cavestomp to play the festival in 1999. Vocalist Jerry Roslie rejected the idea, but Weiss kept pestering the band for the next few years. Roslie, Larry Parypa (guitar) and Rob Lind (sax) finally reformed the band with Ricky Lynn Johnson on drums and Don Wilhelm on bass and began rehearsing in secret. They had no idea that The Sonics had such a fanatical following among garage rockers, and it took them some time to work up the courage to appear at the 2007 Cavestomp. To the band's surprise, the crowd reacted as if they were witnessing the second coming of The Beatles, and The Sonics have been busy ever since.[38] In 2008, The Sonics played club and festival dates in London, Spain, Belgium, Sweden and Norway; the following year, they played shows in Seattle; Long Beach, California; and Austin, Texas, at the South by Southwest festival.[39] In 2009, Freddy Dennis replaced bassist Don Wilhelm. To the delight of their growing horde of fans, the group released an EP containing four new songs in 2010. After drummer Johnson was replaced by Dusty Watson, The Sonics entered the studio again in 2014 to record a full-length album; called *This is The Sonics* (2015), the LP has the dirty, energetic, full-bodied sound that people have come to expect from them.[40] To support the new album, The Sonics toured the U.S., and although Roslie and Parypa announced in 2016 that they would no longer tour with the band, a new line-up toured the u.s. again in the spring of 2017.[41] Sadly, bassist/vocalist Dennis suffered two strokes in July,[42] and any future activity by the band looks questionable.

As wonderful as it is to see classic garage bands from the 1960s get a second chance at receiving the praise and recognition they deserve, garage rock will not survive into the future unless the youth of today develop their own grassroots music scenes. Right now, the u.s. has more than its share of garage bands, but they have trouble finding an audience. It appears that most young Americans would rather look at their phones than watch a band, and the ones who do care about music listen to hip-hop, contemporary country or *American Idol*-style pop; they have no more interest in rock 'n' roll than they would in the weather patterns on Saturn, and American garage bands often have to travel to Europe to find audiences, possibly because Europeans often appreciate American roots music more than Americans do.

In fact, a retro-rock renaissance is happening right now in Europe, where it seems as if the imagery and sounds of the '80s garage revival never went away. One of the hotspots is Spain, with most bands being part of the Famèlic ('the hungry') music collective. Many Spanish bands also adore America's Thee Oh Sees, and what they lack in originality they make up for in exuberance. In the Madrid scene, the top bands are The Parrots and the all-girl Hinds; both bands play basic, familiar chord progressions with clean, reverb-laden guitars, but they stand out by singing with youthful abandon. Other bands in this scene include Los Nastys, Cosmen Adelaida and Lois. The dominant sound in Barcelona is New Wave and/or power pop, and listening to the surf guitars and harmony vocals of Mujere or the jangly power pop of Beach Beach is like travelling back to 1981 to hear Britain's Barracudas. A couple of other bands in the Barcelona scene are Regalim and L'Hereu Escampa.[43]

A much more fuzz-driven sound prevails in Austria, where The Incredible Staggers rule. In terms of their modus operandi,

Like several other '60s garage bands, The Sonics reunited in the 21st century for another shot at playing rock 'n' roll. Here, The Sonics are seen performing at the Double Door in Chicago in 2014.

The Staggers are a Farfisa organ/Vox guitar/fuzz box/pageboy haircut kind of band, and they combine the horror-movie imagery of The Fuzztones with the snottiness of The Gravedigger Five. Their Facebook page explains that the band chooses 'to look like American teen delinquents from the mid-sixties' because they have found that 'Teenage Trash Insanity' is the only way to counteract 'the 21st century's disappearance up its own bland backside'.[44] Most Euro-garage musicians undoubtedly feel the same way.

Of all the underground scenes in Europe, none seems to be as prolific as the one in Switzerland, where bands such as The Come 'n' Go, The Giant Robots, The Shit, The Revox and The Staches are laying down primal rhythms and fuzzed-out riffs. However, the hottest garage band in Switzerland and probably all of Europe is The

Jackets, a trio that puts on high-energy stage shows while playing a blend of '60s garage, Mod, freakbeat and '70s punk. Their guitarist/vocalist, Jack (Jackie) Torera, has a commanding presence onstage, usually wearing Alice Cooper-style make-up around her eyes as she belts out her lyrics and down-and-dirty riffs. The band has played throughout Western Europe, including the UK and Scandinavia, at such festivals as Hipsville (UK), Funtastic Dracula Carnival (Spain), Purple Weekend (Spain), Cosmic Trip Festival (France) and Festival Beat (Italy). Moreover, The Jackets toured the U.S. and Canada in autumn 2017.[45] A similar but less seasoned trio is The Maggie's Marshmallows of Prague, Czech Republic. They play at a more basic level than The Jackets, but they look the part: the bassist/vocalist's long, straight hair covers her eyes as she sings, the guitarist plays a Vox and wears Mod clothes and the drummer looks like a caveman.

Even with all this activity, it would be natural to wonder about the future of garage rock. For how much longer will young hipsters be interested in emulating American teenagers from the mid-twentieth century, playing styles of music that are long detached from their cultural relevance? After all, we are in a post-rock era. As Paul Gambaccini of the BBC explains, the rock era is over in the way that the jazz era is over. Rock musicians will continue to play for enthusiasts in the way that jazz musicians continue to play for a select coterie, but Gambaccini observes that 'rock as a prevailing style is part of music history.'[46] The obvious response to this thought is that as long as youngsters want to make noise with electric guitars and drums, garage rock will survive.

Some promising signs that support this notion are coming out of St Petersburg, Russia, where a grassroots, do-it-yourself scene is taking place, with local bands releasing their recordings on cassette tape. One of the leading groups in this *tusovka* (scene) is Ruka Docheri (Daughter's Hand), an all-girl post-punk outfit that plays dark, dreamy, guitar-based rock. Their home base is a tiny bar called Cliché, one of the main venues for the local garage *tusovka*. It is here that Nastya, the drummer, also sells records from the Garage Karma Store. Nothing more than a sticker-covered cabinet on the wall of Cliché, Garage Karma carries records by local bands, and most of the product consists of cassette tapes released by labels such as Valenton Records, Hair Del, Saint Brooklynsburg and Loser Pop. A cottage industry has grown up around this scene; much of the cover art for the tapes is handmade, and the factory that mass-produces the cassettes, called Go Tape (or GotApe), is based in St Petersburg. People in this scene also maintain contact with garage bands throughout Russia as well as Belarus and Ukraine, and Garage Karma receives orders from as far away as Vladivostok.[47]

The St Petersburg *tusovka* demonstrates that garage rock can thrive in a self-sustaining, self-contained environment that is created by the participants themselves. Local bands such as Ruka Docheri, Bong Rips and Otstoy (Crap) organize their own shows at bars like Cliché and underground clubs like Ionoteka. They keep the prices for admission, drinks and tapes as low as possible so that students and bohemian types can afford to participate. These teenagers and twenty-somethings in St Petersburg have learned that they can do everything themselves with some guitars, tape recorders and blank cassettes, with no help from major record labels, corporate sponsors or mass media. They also show no concern over the idea that their activities could be considered old school or out of fashion. When the members of Ruka Docheri are told that guitar-based rock is not as cool as it was ten years ago, the young women shrug and reply that guitar music will always be cool.[48]

Let's hope that they are right.

References

Introduction

1 Cub Koda, Booklet, *Rock Instrumental Classics, Volume 1: The Fifties*, Rhino Records R2 71601, 1994, compact disc, p. 14.
2 Dan Forte, Booklet, *Twang Thang: The Duane Eddy Anthology*, Rhino Records R2 71223, 1993, compact disc, p. 11.
3 Charlie Gillett, *The Sound of the City: The Rise of Rock and Roll*, 2nd edn (New York, 1996), p. 99.
4 Forte, *Twang Thang*, p. 13.
5 Booklet, *Have 'Twangy' Guitar – Will Travel*, Jamie/Guyden 4007-2, 1999, compact disc, p. 5.
6 Forte, *Twang Thang*, p. 5.
7 Miles Morrisseau, 'Link Wray's Influence on Greatest Rock Guitarists of All Time', www.music.cbc.ca, 29 January 2012.
8 Wayne Janck and Tad Lathrop, *Cult Rockers* (New York, 1995), p. 330.
9 Morrisseau, 'Link Wray's Influence'.
10 Robert Fontenot, '*American Bandstand* Timeline', www.about.com, accessed 19 June 2015.
11 '*American Bandstand*', www.tv.com, accessed 30 June 2015.
12 See Glenn C. Altschuler, *All Shook Up: How Rock 'n' Roll Changed America* (New York, 2004), pp. 152–60.
13 Nina Leibman, 'Nelson, Ozzie and Harriet', *Encyclopedia of Television, Museum of Broadcast Communications*, www.museum.tv, accessed 11 July 2015.
14 Ibid.
15 'The Switched-on Market, How to Turn Up Your Volume', *Billboard* (1 July 1967), p. ws-47, www.books.google.com, accessed 13 July 2015.
16 'Guitars Still Boom', *Billboard* (27 August 1966), p. 68, www.books.google.com, accessed 13 July 2015.
17 Quoted in Tony Bacon, *Echo and Twang: Classic Guitar Music* (San Francisco, CA, 1996), p. 6.

18 Ibid.

19 'Guitars Still Boom', p. 68.

20 Peter Blecha, *Sonic Boom: The History of Northwest Rock, from 'Louie Louie' to 'Smells Like Teen Spirit'* (New York, 2009), pp. 35–6.

21 Ibid., p. 36.

22 Ibid., p. 37.

23 Ibid., p. 63.

24 Ibid., p. 64.

25 Ibid., p. 65.

26 Dave Burke and Alan Taylor, Booklet, *The Fabulous Wailers: The Original Golden Crest Masters*, Ace Records CDCHD 675, 1998, compact disc.

27 Blecha, *Sonic Boom*, p. 66.

28 Ibid., p. 64.

29 Ibid., p. 67.

30 Ibid., p. 114.

31 Quoted ibid., p. 68.

32 Ibid., p. 69.

33 Alec Palao, Booklet, *The Fabulous Wailers: At the Castle | & Co.*, Ace Records CDWIKD 228, 2003, compact disc, p. 4.

34 Blecha, *Sonic Boom*, p. 112.

35 Palao, *The Fabulous Wailers*, p. 5.

36 Ibid., pp. 9–10.

37 Simon Frith, *Sound Effects: Youth, Leisure, and the Politics of Rock'n'Roll*, 2nd edn (New York, 1981), p. 16.

38 Quoted in Palao, *The Fabulous Wailers*, p. 7.

39 Blecha, *Sonic Boom*, p. 41.

40 Ibid., p. 40.

41 Ibid., p. 114.

42 Palao, *The Fabulous Wailers*, p. 5.

43 Blecha, *Sonic Boom*, pp. 115–16.

44 Peter Blecha, 'Etiquette Rules! The Northwest's Reigning '60s Garage-Rock Record Company', www.historylink.org, accessed 19 July 2015.

1 The Founders: American Garage Rock before the Beatles Invasion

1 Don J. Hibbard and Carol Kaleialoha, *The Role of Rock* (Englewood Cliffs, NJ, 1983), p. 7.

2 Jeremy Larner, 'What Do They Get from Rock-'n'-Roll?', *Atlantic Monthly*, CCXIV/2 (1964), pp. 44–9.

3 Ibid., p. 47.

4 Ibid., p. 45.

5 Simon Frith, *Sound Effects: Youth, Leisure, and the Politics of Rock'n'Roll*, 2nd edn (New York, 1981), p. 19.

6 James S. Coleman, *The Adolescent Society: The Social Life of the Teenager and its Impact on Education* (New York, 1961), pp. 13, 23 and 174.

7 See Charlie Gillett, *The Sound of the City: The Rise of Rock and Roll*, 2nd edn (New York, 1996), p. 312.

8 Ron Hall, *Playing for a Piece of the Door: A History of Garage and Frat Bands in Memphis, 1960–1975* (Memphis, TN, 2001), pp. 142–3.

9 Peter Blecha, *Sonic Boom: The History of Northwest Rock, from 'Louie Louie' to 'Smells Like Teen Spirit'* (New York, 2009), p. 161.

10 Ibid., p. 39.

11 Ibid., p. 18.

12 Peter Blecha, 'The Godfather of Northwest Rock and the King of Seattle R&B', www.greenmonkeyrecords.com, January 2006.

13 'Frantics – Seattle (1955–1966)', www.pnwbands.com, accessed 19 February 2016.

14 Ibid.

15 Larry Parypa, Liner Notes, *This is . . . The Savage Young Sonics*, Norton Records NW 909, 2001, vinyl LP.

16 Blecha, *Sonic Boom*, p. 170.

17 Parypa, *Savage Young Sonics*.

18 Ibid.

19 Blecha, *Sonic Boom*, pp. 172–3. See also Pat Long, 'The Psycho Five', in *Shindig! Presents Psychotic Reaction: The U.S. '60s Garage Explosion*, ed. Andy Morten and Jon 'Mojo' Mills (Maidenhead, 2009), pp. 14–15.

20 Long, 'Psycho Five', p. 14.

21 Ibid., p. 16.

22 Ibid., pp. 16–17.

23 Ibid., p. 17.

24 Steven Rosen, 'Might the Sonics Be the Great American Rock Band?', www.huffingtonpost.com, accessed 2 March 2016.

25 Blecha, *Sonic Boom*, pp. 169 and 178.

26 Dave Marsh, *Louie Louie* (New York, 1993), pp. 85–6.

27 Ibid., p. 87.

28 Ibid., p. 81. See also Blecha, *Sonic Boom*, pp. 134–5.

29 Marsh, *Louie Louie*, p. 88.

30 Ibid., pp. 97–100.

31 Ibid., pp. 100–101.

32 Ibid., pp. 107–9.

33 Ibid., pp. 124–5.

34 Ibid., p. 112.

35 Vernon Joynson, *Fuzz, Acid and Flowers Revisited: A Comprehensive Guide to American Garage, Psychedelic, and Hippie Rock, 1964–1975* (London, 2007), p. 514.

36 Blecha, *Sonic Boom*, p. 122.

37 Ibid., pp. 122–3.

38 Ibid., p. 123.

39 Joynson, *Fuzz, Acid and Flowers*, p. 790.

40 Blecha, *Sonic Boom*, p. 124.

41 Ibid., pp. 124–6.

42 Ibid., p. 135.

43 Ibid., pp. 136–8.

44 Ibid., p. 141.

45 Ibid., pp. 142 and 147.

46 Ibid., pp. 145–7.

47 Domenic Priore, 'The Tall Cool Tale of Paul Revere and the Raiders: A Conversation with Mark Lindsay and Paul Revere', www.sundazed.com, 24 March 2011.

48 Gillett, *Sound of the City*, p. 326.

49 Domenic Priore, *Riot on Sunset Strip: Rock'n'Roll's Last Stand in Hollywood* (London, 2007), p. 58.

50 Kent Crowley, *Surf Beat: Rock'n'Roll's Forgotten Revolution* (New York, 2011), pp. 44–5.

51 Ibid., pp. 45–6.

52 Ibid., p. 46.

53 Priore, *Riot on Sunset Strip*, p. 59. See also Greg Shaw, 'The Birth of Surf', in *Bomp! 2: Born in the Garage*, ed. Mike Stax and Suzy Shaw (Burbank, CA, 2009), p. 212.

54 Robert J. Dalley, *Surfin' Guitars: Instrumental Surf Bands of the Sixties*, 2nd edn (Ann Arbor, MI, 1996), p. xv.

55 Priore, *Riot on Sunset Strip*, p. 59.

56 John Blair, 'Dick Dale: The Man Who Invented Surf Music', in *Bomp! 2*, p. 213.

57 Dalley, *Surfin' Guitars*, p. xvi.

58 Priore, *Riot on Sunset Strip*, p. 59.

59 Crowley, *Surf Beat*, p. 78.

60 Ibid., pp. 78–9.

61 Michael Hicks, *Sixties Rock: Garage, Psychedelic, and Other Satisfactions* (Urbana, IL, 1999), p. 68.

62 Crowley, *Surf Beat*, p. 64.
63 Steve Holgate, 'Guitarist Dick Dale Brought Arabic Folk Song to Surf Music', *The Washington File*, Bureau of International Information Programs, U.S. Department of State, 14 September 2006.
64 Arnold Rypens, 'Misirlou', www.originals.be, accessed 19 May 2016.
65 'Misirlou', *Fender Players Club: Dick Dale*, www.fenderplayersclub. com, accessed 19 May 2016.
66 Jim Pewter, Booklet, *Dick Dale and His Del-Tones: Greatest Hits, 1961–1976*, GNP Crescendo Records GNPD 2095, 1992, compact disc, p. 2.
67 Dalley, *Surfin' Guitars*, pp. 111–12.
68 See The Hondells, *Go Little Honda*, Mercury Records MG 20940, 1964, vinyl LP.
69 Priore, *Riot on Sunset Strip*, p. 61.
70 Billy Miller, 'Stompin' All the Way to the Bank', *Kicks*, 7 (1992), p. 17.
71 Billy Miller, 'Billy Talks with Mike Waggoner and the Bops', *Kicks*, 7 (1992), p. 17.
72 Quoted ibid.
73 Billy Miller, 'The Papa Oom Mow Mow Whoa Dad Bird Dance Beat of The Trashmen', *Kicks*, 7 (1992), p. 9.
74 Ibid.
75 Quoted ibid.
76 Joynson, *Fuzz, Acid, and Flowers*, p. 978.
77 Jim Oldsberg, 'Minnetonka's Abominable Snowmen: The Yetti-Men', *Lost and Found*, 2 (1993), pp. 77–8.
78 Oldsberg, 'Minnetonka's Abominable Snowmen', p. 78.
79 Joynson, *Fuzz, Acid and Flowers*, p. 686.
80 Quoted in Jim Oldsberg, 'The Fabulous Jades', *Lost and Found*, 2 (1993), p. 7.
81 Miller, 'The Papa Oom Mow Mow', p. 14.
82 Ibid., p. 13.
83 Ibid., p. 11.
84 Ibid., p. 10.
85 Ibid., p. 13; Jim Oldsberg, 'Rogues Gallery', *Lost and Found*, 2 (1993), p. 131.
86 Peter Roller, *Milwaukee Garage Bands: Generations of Grassroots Rock* (Charleston, SC, 2013), p. 29.
87 Ibid., p. 23.
88 Ibid., pp. 23–5.

89 Joynson, *Fuzz, Acid and Flowers*, p. 537.
90 Mark Prellberg, 'Rockin' 'Round the Valley – The '60s Fox Cities Scene', *Lost and Found*, 2 (1993), p. 38.
91 Ibid., p. 43.
92 Jim Oldsberg, '"Ad Libbing" with The Galaxies', *Lost and Found*, 2 (1993), pp. 90–91.
93 Ibid., pp. 93–5.
94 Ibid., p. 96.
95 Jim Bartels, 'Lenny & The Thundertones', *Kicks*, 7 (1992), p. 72.
96 See www.billboard.com, accessed 30 May 2016.

2 The Creators: The Garage-Rock Supernova in Mid-1960s America

1 David P. Szatmary, *Rockin' in Time: A Social History of Rock-and-Roll*, 6th edn (Upper Saddle River, NJ, 2007), pp. 110–11.
2 Ibid., p. 111.
3 Jack Parr, 'A Look Back: The Beatles' First American Television Appearance', www.youtube.com, accessed 4 June 2016.
4 Szatmary, *Rockin' in Time*, p. 112.
5 Ibid., pp. 101–2.
6 Ibid., p. 103.
7 Ron Hall, *Playing for a Piece of the Door: A History of Garage and Frat Bands in Memphis, 1960–1975* (Memphis, TN, 2001), p. 116.
8 Quoted in Mike Markesich, *Teenbeat Mayhem! Commemorating America's Forgotten Musical Heritage: Those Teenage Rock and Roll Combos of the Swingin' 1960s* (Branford, CT, 2012), p. 12.
9 Ibid.
10 Quoted in GONN, Booklet *Frenzology, 1966–1967: Punks along the Mississippi*, MCCM Records MCCM CD 9601, 1996, compact disc.
11 Quoted in Michael Hicks, *Sixties Rock: Garage, Psychedelic, and Other Satisfactions* (Urbana, IL, 1999), p. 25.
12 Ibid.
13 Mark Prellberg, 'Rockin' 'Round the Valley', p. 37. See also Peter Roller, *Milwaukee Garage Bands: Generations of Grassroots Rock* (Charleston, SC, 2013), p. 29.
14 Hall, *Playing for a Piece of the Door*, p. 9.
15 'Teen-age Money Music', *Life*, LX/2 (1966), p. 103, www.books.google.com, accessed 13 July 2015; 'The Switched-on Market, How to Turn Up Your Volume', *Billboard* (1 July 1967), p. ws-47, www.books.google.com, accessed 13 July 2015. See Introduction, p. 14.

16 Charlie Gillett, *The Sound of the City: The Rise of Rock and Roll,* 2nd edn (New York, 1996), pp. 313–14.

17 Hall, *Playing for a Piece of the Door,* p. 72.

18 Vernon Joynson, *Fuzz, Acid and Flowers: A Comprehensive Guide to American Garage, Psychedelic, and Hippie Rock, 1964–1975* (London, 2004), p. 168. See also Markesich, *TeenBeat Mayhem!,* p. 13.

19 Joynson, *Fuzz, Acid and Flowers,* p. 116. See also Markesich, *TeenBeat Mayhem!,* p. 13.

20 Joynson, *Fuzz, Acid and Flowers,* p. 19. See also Markesich, *TeenBeat Mayhem!,* p. 13.

21 Mike Stax, 'Optical Sound: The Technicolor Tales Behind the Numerous Nuggets', Booklet, *Nuggets: Original Artyfacts from the First Psychedelic Era, 1965–1968,* Rhino R2 75466, 1998, boxed set of compact discs, p. 32.

22 Jon Stratton, 'Englishing Popular Music in the 1960s', in *Britpop and the English Music Tradition,* ed. Andy Bennett and Jon Stratton (Farnham, 2010), p. 43.

23 Stratton, 'Skiffle, Variety and Englishness', in *Britpop and the English Music Tradition,* ed. Andy Bennett and Jon Stratton (Farnham, 2010), p. 32.

24 Gillett, *The Sound of the City,* p. 259.

25 Alan Clayson, *The Beat Merchants: The Origins, History, Impact and Rock Legacy of the 1960s British Pop Groups* (London, 1995), pp. 30–31.

26 Ibid., p. 78.

27 Stratton, 'Englishing Popular Music in the 1960s', p. 44.

28 Joynson, *Fuzz, Acid and Flowers,* p. 407.

29 Ibid., p. 531.

30 Ibid., p. 730.

31 Ibid., p. 154.

32 Ibid., p. 362.

33 Ibid., p. 370.

34 Ibid., pp. 994–5.

35 Peter Blecha, *Sonic Boom: The History of Northwest Rock, from 'Louie Louie' to 'Smells Like Teen Spirit'* (New York, 2009), p. 30.

36 Alec Palao, Booklet, *The Fabulous Wailers: At the Castle | & Co.,* Big Beat CDWIKD 228, 2003, compact disc.

37 Szatmary, *Rockin' in Time,* p. 122.

38 Richie Unterberger, *Urban Spacemen and Wayfaring Strangers: Overlooked Innovators and Eccentric Visionaries of '60s Rock* (San Francisco, CA, 2000), pp. 126–7.

39 Quoted in Szatmary, *Rockin' in Time*, p. 123.

40 Michael Hicks, *Sixties Rock: Garage, Psychedelic, and Other Satisfactions* (Urbana, IL, 1999), p. 30.

41 Ibid., p. 30.

42 Ibid., p. 29. See also Dave Laing, *One Chord Wonders: Power and Meaning in Punk Rock* (Oakland, CA, 2015), p. 79.

43 Ibid., p. 28.

44 Ibid., p. 31.

45 Seth Bovey, '"Don't Tread on Me": The Ethos of '60s Garage Punk', *Popular Music and Society*, XXIX/4 (2006), p. 456.

46 George R. White, *Bo Diddley: Living Legend* (Chessington, 1995), p. 137.

47 Ibid., pp. 144–5.

48 Gillett, *Sound of the City*, p. 337. See also Dominic Priore, *Riot on Sunset Strip: Rock'n'Roll's Last Stand in Hollywood* (London, 2007), p. 74.

49 Szatmary, *Rockin' in Time*, p. 100.

50 Gillett, *Sound of the City*, p. 338.

51 Szatmary, *Rockin' in Time*, pp. 98 and 100. See also Priore, *Riot on Sunset Strip*, p. 76.

52 Szatmary, *Rockin' in Time*, p. 98.

53 Priore, *Riot on Sunset Strip*, p. 78. See also Gillett, *Sound of the City*, p. 338.

54 Unterberger, *Urban Spacemen and Wayfaring Strangers*, pp. 174–5.

55 Ibid., pp. 175–6.

56 Ibid., p. 176.

57 Joynson, *Fuzz, Acid and Flowers*, p. 63.

58 Ibid., p. 97.

59 Richie Unterberger, *Unknown Legends of Rock'n'Roll: Psychedelic Unknowns, Mad Geniuses, Punk Pioneers, Lo-fi Mavericks, and More* (San Francisco, CA, 1998), p. 326.

60 Ibid., pp. 326–7. See also Joynson, *Fuzz, Acid and Flowers*, p. 97.

61 Markesich, *TeenBeat Mayhem!*, p. 14.

62 Some good examples of jangle-beat include 'Who Do You Think You're Foolin' by The Disillusioned Younger Generation, a group from California; 'I'm Always Doing Something Wrong' by The Fab Four of Kansas City, Missouri; 'Can You' by Sir Michael and the Sounds of Clearwater, Florida; 'I Cannot Lie' by The Zone V of Shickshinny, Pennsylvania; 'Shame' by The Kings Ransom of Allentown, Pennsylvania; 'I'm Really Sorry' by The JuJus of Grand Rapids, Michigan; and 'Hey Girl' by Lime of Akron, Ohio.

63 For a complete account of the origins and history of 'Hey Joe', see Hicks, *Sixties Rock*, pp. 39–57.
64 Hicks, *Sixties Rock*, pp. 19–20.
65 Ibid., p. 14.
66 Ibid., p. 17.
67 Ibid., pp. 21–2.
68 Ed Sanders, *Fug You* (Philadelphia, PA, 2011), p. 404.
69 Quoted in Markesich, *TeenBeat Mayhem!*, p. 294.
70 Lenny Kaye, Liner Notes, *Nuggets: Original Artyfacts from the First Psychedelic Era, 1965–1968*, Elektra 7E 2006, 1972, vinyl LP.
71 Quoted in Laing, *One Chord Wonders*, pp. 21–2.
72 Quoted in Hicks, *Sixties Rock*, p. 19.
73 Markesich, *TeenBeat Mayhem!*, p. 295.
74 Bovey, 'The Ethos of '60s Garage Punk', p. 452.
75 Hicks, *Sixties Rock*, p. 26.
76 Ibid., p. 27.
77 Bovey, 'The Ethos of '60s Garage Punk', p. 453.
78 Other examples include The Mile Ends' 'Bottle Up and Go', The 13th Floor Elevators' 'You're Gonna Miss Me', The Zachary Thaks' 'Bad Girl', The We Fews' 'Surprise Surprise' and The Bad Roads' 'Too Bad' and 'Blue Girl', ibid., pp. 453–4.
79 Greg Shaw, '"Sic Transit Gloria . . .": The Story of Punk Rock in the '60s', Booklet, *Nuggets: Original Artyfacts from the First Psychedelic Era, 1965–1968*, Rhino R2 75466, 1998, boxed set of compact discs.
80 Bovey, 'The Ethos of '60s Garage Punk', p. 455.
81 Anja Stax, 'The Pleasure Seekers', *Ugly Things*, 31 (2011), pp. 55–6.
82 Ibid., pp. 56–7.
83 Quoted ibid., p. 57.
84 Ibid., p. 56.
85 Quoted ibid., pp. 58–9.
86 Markesich, *TeenBeat Mayhem!*, p. 289.
87 Joynson, *Fuzz, Acid and Flowers*, p. 197.
88 Ibid., p. 70.
89 Ibid., p. 228.
90 Ibid., p. 1049.
91 Ibid., p. 81.
92 Ibid., p. 310.
93 'Teen-age Money Music', p. 106.
94 Hicks, *Sixties Rock*, pp. 63–4.
95 Ibid., p. 64.
96 Ibid., p. 65.

97 Ibid., pp. 66–9.
98 Ann Johnson and Mike Stax, 'From Psychotic to Psychedelic: The Garage Contribution to Psychedelia', *Popular Music and Society*, XXIX/4 (2006), p. 418.
99 Bovey, 'The Ethos of '60s Garage Punk', pp. 456–7.
100 Joynson, *Fuzz, Acid and Flowers*, p. 965.
101 Markesich, *TeenBeat Mayhem!*, p. 36.
102 Ibid.
103 Ibid., p. 50.

3 The World Beaters: The British Invasion and the Beat Heard 'Round the World

1 Except in the U.S., where music fans already had The Ventures and many other instrumental rock combos to listen to.
2 Richard Dawkins, *The Selfish Gene* (Oxford, 1999), pp. 189–201.
3 Fernando Salaverri, *Sólo éxitos: año a año, 1959–2002* (Madrid, 2005), n.p.
4 Randal Wood, Booklet, *Los Nuggetz: '60s Garage and Psych from Latin America*, RockBeat Records ROC-CD 3073, 2013, boxed set of compact discs, pp. 19 and 32.
5 Ibid., pp. 14–15.
6 Ibid., pp. 9 and 26.
7 Ibid., pp. 19 and 20.
8 Ibid., p. 7.
9 Jason Ankeny, 'Los Dug Dug's', www.allmusic.com, accessed 8 August 2017.
10 Wood, *Los Nuggetz*, p. 42.
11 Ankeny, 'Los Dug Dug's'.
12 Wood, *Los Nuggetz*, p. 42.
13 Ibid., p. 20.
14 Ibid., p. 11.
15 Richie Unterberger, 'Los Shakers', www.allmusic.com, accessed 4 August 2017.
16 'The Uruguayan Invasion', www.uruguaynow.com, accessed 3 August 2017.
17 Wood, *Los Nuggetz*, pp. 20–21.
18 'The Uruguayan Invasion', www.uruguaynow.com.
19 Richie Unterberger, 'Los Mockers', www.allmusic.com, accessed 4 August 2017.
20 Wood, *Los Nuggetz*, p. 44.

21 Unterberger, 'Los Mockers'.
22 Mark Deming, 'Los Gatos Salvajes', www.allmusic.com, accessed 5 August 2017.
23 Pablo Alabarces, *Entre gatos y violadores: el rock nacional en la cultura argentina* (Buenos Aires, 1993), pp. 45–50.
24 Fidel Gutierrez Mendoza, 'Wildmen in the City: A Story About Los Saicos', Booklet, *Los Saicos: ¡Demolicion!: The Complete Recordings*, Munster Records Distolux SL, 2010, compact disc, p. 10.
25 Ibid., p. 21.
26 See Jonathan Watts and Dan Collyns, 'Where Did Punk Begin? A Cinema in Peru', www.theguardian.com, 14 September 2012. See also Katherine Brooks, 'Meet Los Saicos, The Peruvian Band Credited with Inventing Punk Rock', www.huffingtonpost.com, 15 August 2013, and Martin Schneider, 'If Peru's Los Saicos Aren't the First Punk Band, They're Pretty Close', www.dangerousminds. net, 26 August 2013.
27 Wood, *Los Nuggetz*, p. 7.
28 Ibid., p. 22.
29 Ibid., p. 7.
30 Miriam Linna, Liner Notes, *The Great Lost Trashmen Album*, Sundazed LP 5003, 1990, vinyl LP.
31 Wood, *Los Nuggetz*, pp. 7, 13 and 59.
32 Ibid., p. 13.
33 Ibid., p. 59.
34 Hugo Taylor, 'Speaking of the Speakers', *Ugly Things*, 22 (2004), p. 106.
35 Wood, *Los Nuggetz*, p. 33.
36 Taylor, 'Speaking of the Speakers', p. 107.
37 John Bush, 'Os Mutantes', www.allmusic.com, accessed 13 August 2017.
38 Wood, *Los Nuggetz*, p. 10.
39 Billy Miller, 'The Papa Oom Mow Mow Whoa Dad Bird Dance Beat of The Trashmen', *Kicks*, 7 (1992), pp. 11–12.
40 Tim Warren, Booklet, *Last of the Garage Punk Unknowns: Volumes 5 and 6*, Crypt Records Crypt-116, n.d., compact disc.
41 Greg Shaw, Liner Notes, *Pebbles, Volume 18: The Continent Lashes Back! European Garage Rock Part 2*, Archive International Productions AIP 10033, 1985, vinyl LP.
42 Terry Waghorne, 'Pirate Radio in the UK', *BOMP! 2: Born in the Garage*, ed. Mike Stax and Suzy Shaw (n.p., UT Publishing, 2009), p. 152.
43 Shaw, Liner Notes, *Pebbles, Volume 18*.

44 Pim Scheelings, 'The Motions . . . in Motion', *Ugly Things*, 36 (2013), p. 35.
45 Mike Stax, 'The Life I Live: Q65, The Outsiders, and the Dutch Beat Revolution', *Ugly Things*, 45 (2017), p. 10. See also Casper Roos, 'The Continuing Story of Golden Earring – The Sixties', www.members. ziggo.nl/casper.roos, accessed 21 August 2017.
46 See Scheelings, 'The Motions . . . in Motion', p. 37.
47 Ibid., pp. 37–8.
48 Casper Roos, 'The Continuing Story of Golden Earring'.
49 Steve Huey, 'Golden Earring', www.allmusic.com, accessed 21 August 2017.
50 Richie Unterberger, 'Inside the Outsiders: Story One: The Wally Tax Interview', *Ugly Things*, 16 (1998), p. 87.
51 Stax, 'The Life I Live', p. 9.
52 Ibid., p. 11.
53 Unterberger, 'Inside the Outsiders', p. 87.
54 Ibid., p. 12.
55 Stax, 'The Life I Live', p. 13.
56 Ibid., pp. 8 and 11.
57 Ibid., pp. 18–19.
58 Ibid., p. 23.
59 Mike Stax, Review of *Otto & Die Beatle Jungs* by Hans-Jurgen Klitsch, *Ugly Things*, 28 (2009), p. 25.
60 Richie Unterberger, 'The Lords', www.allmusic.com, accessed 24 August 2017.
61 Mike Stax, Review of *In Black and White, In Beat and Sweet* by The Lords, *Ugly Things*, 30 (2010), p. 148.
62 Greg Shaw, 'Rockin' around the World', BOMP! *2: Born in the Garage*, ed. Suzy Shaw and Mike Stax (n.p., UT Publishing, 2009), p. 149.
63 See Gregor Kessler, 'The Loosers: Krauts on the Loose', *Ugly Things*, 37 (2014), pp. 139–41. See also Anja Bungert, 'The Tiles: Beat an der Saar', *Ugly Things*, 17 (1999), pp. 73–4.
64 Quoted in Mike Stax, Booklet, *Black Monk Time*, Infinite Zero 9 43112-2, 1997, compact disc, p. 10.
65 Quoted ibid., p. 5.
66 Richie Unterberger, *Unknown Legends of Rock 'n' Roll: Psychedelic Unknowns, Mad Geniuses, Punk Pioneers, Lo-fi Mavericks and More* (San Francisco, CA, 1998), p. 348.
67 Stax, *Black Monk Time*, p. 12.
68 Unterberger, *Unknown Legends*, pp. 350–51.

69 Ibid.

70 Greg Shaw and Lennart Persson, 'Sounds of the Sixties, Part Four: Sweden', BOMP! 2: Born in the Garage, ed. Suzy Shaw and Mike Stax (n.p., UT Publishing, 2009), p. 270.

71 Ibid., p. 271. See also Lenny Helsing, Review of Tages – Go! The Complete Singles, RPM International, UK, 2015, 2 compact discs, Ugly Things, 40 (2015), p. 147.

72 Shaw and Persson, 'Sounds of the Sixties, Part Four: Sweden', p. 271.

73 Ibid., p. 272.

74 Ibid., p. 273.

75 Mike Stax, 'Danish Beat: Cool Like Frost', Ugly Things, 22 (2004), p. 192.

76 See the artists' biographies at www.rockipedia.no/artister, accessed 1 September 2017.

77 Mike Stax, 'The Dandy Girls, Part 1: Teenage Girl-next-door Rock 'n' Roll', Ugly Things, 27 (2008), p. 163.

78 Ibid., p. 164.

79 Ibid., p. 165.

80 Ibid., pp. 166–7.

81 Ibid., p. 167.

82 Mike Stax with Thor G. Norås, 'The Dandy Girls, Part 2: Guitars, Mascara, and Napalm', Ugly Things, 28 (2009), pp. 65–72.

83 Greg Shaw, Liner Notes, Pebbles, Volume 18: The Continent Lashes Back! European Garage Rock Part 2.

84 Claudio Sorge, 'Ravin' Rokes', Kicks, 1 (1979), pp. 47–8.

85 Beat music did exist behind the Iron Curtain, but an exploration of it is beyond the scope of this book. Interested readers should consult the booklets from the multi-volume compilation series Planetary Pebbles: Surfbeat Behind the Iron Curtain, which collects songs from the German Democratic Republic, Russia, Hungary, Romania and Czechoslovakia. The efforts of musicians in these countries to play rock 'n' roll despite government crackdowns and censorship reveals just how important beat music was to young people all over the world.

86 Mike Stax, 'The Masters Apprentices, Part One: Hands of Time', Ugly Things, 29, pp. 13–14.

87 Ibid., p. 27.

88 Ibid., p. 29.

89 Ibid., p. 18.

90 Ibid., pp. 19 and 22.

91 Ibid., p. 30.

92 Ibid., pp. 37–9.

93 Mike Stax, 'The Masters Apprentices, Part Two: Band Moll Paradise', *Ugly Things*, 30 (2010), p. 109.

94 Greg Shaw, 'The Vanda-Young Story', *BOMP!* 2, p. 284.

95 Bruce Eder, 'The Easybeats', www.allmusic.com, accessed 7 September 2017.

96 Richie Unterberger, 'The Missing Links', www.allmusic.com, accessed 7 September 2017.

97 Andrew Schmidt, 'Andy James: The Missing Link', *Ugly Things*, 17 (1999), p. 29.

98 Ibid., p. 30.

99 Unterberger, 'The Missing Links'.

100 Quoted in Iain McIntyre, 'Chants R&B: Live Witchdoctors', *Ugly Things*, 19 (2001), pp. 49–51.

101 Bruce Sergent, 'Bari and The Breakways', *New Zealand Music of the 60's, 70's and a Bit of 80's*, www.sergent.com.au/music, accessed 13 September 2017.

102 Bruce Sergent, 'La De Das', *New Zealand Music of the 60's, 70's and a Bit of 80's*, www.sergent.com.au/music, accessed 13 September 2017.

103 Bruce Sergent, 'Tom Thumb', *New Zealand Music of the 60's, 70's and a Bit of 80's*, www.sergent.com.au/music, accessed 13 September 2017.

104 Ibid.

105 See 'Historical Periods in Papua New Guinea Music', *Music Archive for Papua New Guinea*, www.hmcs.scu.edu.au/musicarchive, accessed 14 September 2017.

106 Joseph Pereira, 'The Checkmates', *Ugly Things*, 23 (2005), p. 85.

107 Ibid., p. 86.

108 Ibid., p. 87.

109 Ibid., pp. 87–8.

110 Ibid., p. 89.

111 Joseph Clement Pereira, 'The Straydogs', *Ugly Things*, 19 (2001), p. 115.

112 Ibid., p. 116.

113 Ibid., p. 117.

114 'HK Pop History', *Hong Kong Pop: English Style*, www.home.ied.edu. hk/~hkpop, accessed 21 September 2017.

115 'The 60's Popular Music Scene in the Far East', www.questing. wordpress.com, accessed 21 September 2017.

116 Joseph C. Pereira, 'The Quests', *Ugly Things*, 21 (2003), pp. 71–3.

117 Barin-Turica and Stehan Kery, Booklet, *Thai Beat A Go-Go: Volume One*, Subliminal Sounds SUBCD 11, 2004, compact disc.

118 'Weird Psychedelic Soundwaves from Southeast Asia in the 60s and 70s', www.rateyourmusic.com/list/novocaine69, accessed 22 September 2017. See also 'Thailand', *Radiodiffusion Internasionaal Annexe*, www.radiodiffusion.wordpress.com, accessed 22 September 2017.

119 'Thailand', www.radiodiffusion.wordpress.com.

120 Barin-Turica and Kery, Booklet, *Thai Beat A Go-Go, Volume 1*.

121 Ibid.

122 'Thailand', www.radiodiffusion.wordpress.com.

123 Barin-Turica and Kery, *Thai Beat A Go-Go, Volume 1*.

124 Philip Brasor, 'The Ventures: Still Rocking After 50 Years', www.japantimes.co.jp/culture, 7 August 2008.

125 'Japan's Bunnys', *Fancy: Fashion, Art and Crap*, www.fancymag.com, 2005.

126 'The 60's Popular Music Scene in the Far East'.

127 'The Spiders', *Radiodiffusion Internasionaal Annexe*, www.radiodiffusion.wordpress.com, 23 June 2008.

4 The Resurrectors: Bringing 1960s Garage Rock Back from the Grave in the 1970s

1 Although Paul Revere and the Raiders did maintain their popularity into the 1970s, their line-up changed several times, with only Paul Revere and Mark Lindsey being continuing members.

2 Ian Fornam, 'School's Out Forever', *Classic Rock Presents Alice Cooper* (2011), p. 43.

3 Ibid., p. 44.

4 Dave Swanson, 'Fire! Ready! Aim!', in *Shindig! Annual Number Three*, ed. Andy Morten (Maidenhead, n.d.), p. 29.

5 Fornam, 'School's Out Forever', p. 44. See also Swanson, 'Fire! Ready! Aim!', p. 29.

6 Swanson, 'Fire! Ready! Aim!', p. 31.

7 Fornam, 'School's Out Forever', p. 44.

8 Ibid., p. 45.

9 Ibid., pp. 46–7. See also Swanson, 'Fire! Ready! Aim!', pp. 31–2.

10 Swanson, 'Fire! Ready! Aim!', p. 33.

11 Chris Smith, *101 Albums that Changed Popular Music* (New York, 2009), pp. 95–6.

12 John Milward, 'The New York Dolls', in *The Rolling Stone Record Guide*, ed. Dave Marsh with John Swenson (New York, 1979), p. 271.

13 Mike Stax, 'Rock is a Way of Life: Greg Shaw and the Roots of Rock Fandom', in *Bomp! 2: Born in the Garage*, ed. Suzy Shaw and Mike Stax (n.p., UT Publishing, 2009), pp. 13–14.

14 Greg Shaw, 'Prelude to the Morning of an Inventory of the '60s', *Who Put the Bomp*, 6 (1971), p. 9.

15 Ibid., p. 10.

16 Shaw, 'R.I.A.W.O.L.', *Who Put the Bomp*, 6 (1971), pp. 5–6.

17 Dave Marsh, Letter, *Who Put the Bomp*, 6 (1971), p. 38.

18 Lester Bangs, 'Psychotic Reactions and Caburetor Dung: A Tale of These Times', *Psychotic Reactions and Carburetor Dung*, ed. Greil Marcus (New York, 1988), pp. 5 and 8–9.

19 Ibid., p. 9.

20 Ibid., pp. 9–10.

21 Ibid., pp. 13–14 and 15.

22 Ibid., p. 8.

23 Ibid., p. 10.

24 Ibid., pp. 12 and 19.

25 Jac Holzman, 'Ask Me Anything', www.reddit.com, accessed 29 May 2017.

26 Lenny Kaye, www.lennykaye.com, accessed 29 May 2017.

27 Ibid.

28 Mike Markesich, *TeenBeat Mayhem! Commemorating America's Forgotten Musical Heritage: Those Teenage Rock and Roll Combos of the Swingin' 1960s* (Branford, CT, 2012), pp. 38–9.

29 Quoted in Stephen Deusner, 'Punk Pioneer Lenny Kaye Reflects Back on "The Original Sin of Rock 'n' Roll"', www.salon.com, 29 November 2015.

30 Markesich, *TeenBeat Mayhem!*, p. 39.

31 Chris Smith, *101 Albums*, p. 98.

32 Markesich, *TeenBeat Mayhem!*, p. 39.

33 Ibid.

34 Ibid., p. 40.

35 Dave Laing, *One Chord Wonders: Power and Meaning in Punk Rock* (Oakland, CA, 2015), p. 23.

36 Kieron Tyler, 'Track by Track', Booklet, *Children of Nuggets*, Rhino R2 74639, 2005, boxed set of compact discs, p. 46.

37 Markesich, *TeenBeat Mayhem!*, p. 40.

38 'Proto-Punk', www.allmusic.com, accessed 29 May 2017.

39 Vernon Joynson, *Fuzz, Acid and Flowers Revisited: A Comprehensive Guide to American Garage, Psychedelic and Hippie Rock, 1964–1975* (London, 2004), p. 234.
40 Rolf Sempredon, 'Debris', www.allmusic.com, accessed 1 June 2017.
41 Joynson, *Fuzz, Acid and Flowers*, p. 1016.
42 See Jon Savage and Stuart Baker, Booklet, *Punk 45: Sick on You! One Way Spit! After the Love and Before the Revolution, Volume 3: Proto-Punk 1969–76*, Soul Jazz Records SJR CD279, 2014, compact disc.
43 Isabelle Anscombe and Dike Blair, *Punk: Punk Rock/Punk Style/Punk Stance/Punk People/Punk Stars/That Head the New Wave in England and America* (New York, 1978), p. 7.
44 Ibid.
45 Ibid., p. 55.
46 Chris Morris, 'Rock 'n' Roll and Its Discontents', Booklet, *No Thanks! The '70s Punk Rebellion*, Rhino R2 73926, 2003, boxed set of compact discs, p. 25.
47 Greg Shaw, 'In Defense of Rock Theory', BOMP! *Saving the World One Record at a Time*, ed. Suzy Shaw and Mick Farren (n.p., AMMO Books, 2007), p. 186.
48 Ibid., p. 188.
49 Greg Shaw, 'The Beat: Editorial', *BOMP!*, 20 (1979), p. 6.
50 Quoted in Stax, 'Rock is a Way of Life', p. 24

5 The Revivalists: Replaying 1960s Garage Rock in the 1980s and Beyond

1 Greg Shaw, 'Ya Gotta Have Moxie . . .', Booklet, *Ya Gotta Have Moxie: Volume One*, AIP/Moxie Records AIPCD1059, 1998, compact disc, pp. 2–4.
2 See Vernon Joynson, *Fuzz, Acid and Flowers Revisited: A Comprehensive Guide to American Garage, Psychedelic and Hippie Rock, 1964–1975* (London, 2004), pp. 1091–8.
3 This term is borrowed from a 1984 compilation album on Big Beat Records called *Rockabilly Psychosis and the Garage Disease*.
4 See the etymologies of 'garage rock' and 'garage band' at www.english.stackhouse.com, accessed 15 July 2017.
5 Quoted in Markesich, *TeenBeat Mayhem! Commemorating America's Forgotten Musical Heritage: Those Teenage Rock and Roll Combos of the Swingin' 1960s* (Branford, CT, 2012), p. 294.
6 Ibid., p. 42.
7 Mike Stax, 'I Joined the Voxx Rebellion and I Didn't Even Get a Lousy T-shirt', *Bomp! Saving the World One Record at a Time*,

ed. Suzy Shaw and Mick Farren (n.p., AMMO Books, 2007), pp. 258–61. See also Timothy Gassen, 'It Was Thirty Years Ago Today? A History of Garage and Psychedelic Music in the 1980s and 1990s', *The Knights of Fuzz: The Garage and Psychedelic Music Explosion, 1980–2000*, Purple Cactus Media Productions PCMP2001, 2001,

CD-ROM, p. 4.

8 Stax, 'I Joined the Voxx Rebellion', p. 261. See also Gassen, 'It Was Thirty Years Ago Today?', p. 5.

9 Gassen, 'It Was Thirty Years Ago Today?', pp. 4–5.

10 Ibid., p. 5.

11 Rich Coffee, 'Thee Fourgiven: It Ain't Pretty Down Here', Booklet, *It Ain't Pretty Down Here*, Dionysus ID1233128, 2006, compact disc.

12 Stax, 'I Joined the Voxx Rebellion', pp. 259–60.

13 Gassen, 'It Was Thirty Years Ago Today?', p. 8.

14 Stax, 'I Joined the Voxx Rebellion', p. 260.

15 Quoted in Gassen, 'It Was Thirty Years Ago Today?', p. 5.

16 Ibid., p. 8.

17 Ibid.

18 Ibid.

19 Shimmy, 'Midnight Records: Part 2', *Bananas Magazine*, 2 (2010), p. 31.

20 'The Scene', www.cheepskatemovie.com, accessed 6 July 2017.

21 Shimmy, 'Midnight Records: Part 1', *Bananas Magazine*, 1 (2010), pp. 28–9.

22 Shimmy, 'Midnight Records: Part 2', p. 32.

23 Ibid., pp. 30–31.

24 Ibid., p. 32.

25 Gassen, 'It Was Thirty Years Ago Today?', p. 9.

26 Shimmy, 'Midnight Records: Part 2', p. 32.

27 Ibid., pp. 32–3.

28 Herve Columbet, 'The Musicians: Mike Spenser', *The (Count) Bishops*, www.countbishops.free.fr, 2003–5.

29 Nigel Cross, 'Notes from the '80s Underground: How the Guitars Fought Back', Booklet, *Children of Nuggets: Original Artyfacts from the Second Psychedelic Era, 1976–1996*, Rhino R2 74639, 2005, boxed set of compact discs, pp. 15–16.

30 Ibid., p. 16.

31 Ibid.

32 Vernon Joynson, *The Acid Trip: A Complete Guide to Psychedelic Music* (Todmorden, Lancashire, 1984), p. 133.

33 Jim DeRogatis, *Kaleidoscope Eyes*, pp. 161–2.

34 Joynson, *The Acid Trip*, p. 133.
35 Ibid., p. 133.
36 Gassen, 'It Was Thirty Years Ago Today?', pp. 9–10.
37 Joynson, *The Acid Trip*, p. 133.
38 Gassen, 'It Was Thirty Years Ago Today?', p. 11.
39 Cross, 'Notes from the '80s Underground', pp. 16–17.
40 Some of the best revival bands from international scenes include The Cryptones (France), Sex Museum and Los Negativos (Spain), The Broken Jug and Shiny Gnomes (Germany), The Sick Rose and Technicolor Dreams (Italy), The Sound Explosion (Greece), The Other Side and The Kliek (the Netherlands), Cosmic Dropouts and The Lust-O-Rama (Norway) and The Creeps, The Stomachmouths, Watermelon Men, Wylde Mammoths and The Nomads (Sweden). Beyond Europe were The Ten Commandments and The Worst (Canada), The Chills (New Zealand) and The Bo-Weevils, Hoodoo Gurus and Lime Spiders (Australia).
41 See Gassen, *The Knights of Fuzz*, pp. 291–3.
42 Gassen, 'It Was Thirty Years Ago Today?', p. 11.
43 Markesich, *TeenBeat Mayhem!*, p. 42.

6 The Backtrackers: Garage Rock in the Twenty-first Century

1 Mike Markesich, *TeenBeat Mayhem! Commemorating America's Forgotten Musical Heritage: Those Teenage Rock and Roll Combos of the Swingin' 1960s* (Branford, CT, 2012), p. 43.
2 Beverly Bryan, 'Please Explain: What is Garage Punk? How a Retrograde Strain of Weird, Fun Punk Stays Alive in the Underground, or: Are You Bored with Animal Collective Yet?', www.mtviggy.com, 4 February 2013.
3 'Garage Punk', www.allmusic.com, accessed 4 November 2017. See also Markesich, *Teenbeat Mayhem!*, p. 43.
4 Bryan, 'Please Explain'.
5 Quoted ibid.
6 Ibid.
7 Ibid.
8 Everett True, *The White Stripes and the Sound of Mutant Blues* (London, 2004), pp. 34–5. See also Rich Tupica, 'Mick Collins Interview – Talks Gories, Opening for Rob Tyner', *Turn It Down: Interviews with Garage-Punk and Rock-n-Roll Musicians*, www.turnit-down.blogspot.com, 6 April 2013.
9 True, *The White Stripes*, p. 34.

10 Ibid., p. 37.

11 Quoted ibid., p. 36.

12 'Punk Blues', www.allmusic.com, accessed 9 November 2017.

13 Kieron Tyler, 'Track by Track', Booklet, *Children of Nuggets: Original Artyfacts from the Second Psychedelic Era, 1976–1996*, Rhino R2 74639, 2005, boxed set of compact discs, p. 54.

14 Chris Smith, 101 *Albums that Changed Popular Music* (New York, 2009), p. 240. Today's music journalists seem to have forgotten about the commercial success of 1960s garage bands such as Paul Revere and the Raiders.

15 Quoted in Eric Been, '10 Years after The White Stripes "Saved" It, Rock is Again in Crisis', www.theatlantic.com, 5 July 2011.

16 Quoted in True, *The White Stripes*, p. 33.

17 Ibid., p. 56.

18 Ibid., p. 51.

19 Smith, 101 *Albums*, p. 241.

20 Otto Mühl, 'The Black Lips Want to Get You Drunk', www.anthemmagazine.com, 1 May 2007.

21 Mark Deming, 'The Black Lips', www.allmusic.com, accessed 20 October 2017.

22 Steve Leggett, 'Thee Oh Sees', www.allmusic.com, accessed 20 October 2017.

23 Jeff Terich, 'Freedom Rock: The Fuzzbox Liturgy of Ty Segall', www.floodmagazine.com, 20 January 2017.

24 Stephen Thomas Erlewine, 'The Black Keys', www.allmusic.com, accessed 23 November 2017.

25 David Dudley, 'Last Band Standing', AARP: *The Magazine*, LIX/4 (2016), p. 58.

26 Mark Deming, 'The Sloths', www.allmusic.com, accessed 12 November 2017; Dudley, 'Last Band Standing', pp. 56 and 70.

27 Vernon Joynson, *Fuzz, Acid and Flowers Revisited: A Comprehensive Guide to American Garage, Psychedelic and Hippie Rock, 1964–1975* (London, 2004), p. 176.

28 Ibid.

29 Bruce Eder, 'The Chocolate Watchband', www.allmusic.com, accessed 12 November 2017.

30 Joynson, *Fuzz, Acid and Flowers*, p. 176.

31 See www.whiskyagogo.com, accessed 16 November 2017.

32 Eder, 'The Chocolate Watchband'.

33 Will Shade, *The Devolution of Überbeat: A Monks Discography and Videography*, www.the-monks.com, accessed 12 November 2017.

34 Richie Unterberger, *Unknown Legends of Rock 'n' Roll: Psychedelic Unknowns, Mad Geniuses, Punk Pioneers, Lo-fi Mavericks and More* (San Francisco, CA, 1998), p. 353.

35 Jon Pareles, 'The Monks' Moment, Recaptured', www.nytimes.com, 8 November 1999.

36 Whitmore, 'Dave Day in Memoriam', www.amoeba.com, 13 January 2008.

37 Klemen Brezniker, 'Monks Interview with Thomas Shaw', www.psychedelicbaby.blogspot.com, 2011; Andy Matt, 'Gary Burger, 1941–2014', www.completemusicupdate.com, 19 March 2014.

38 Pat Long, 'The Psycho Five', in *Shindig! Presents Psychotic Reaction: The U.S. '60s Garage Explosion*, ed. Andy Morten and Jon 'Mojo' Mills (Maidenhead, 2009), p. 19.

39 See www.thesonicsboom.com, accessed 12 November 2017.

40 Mark Deming, 'The Sonics', www.allmusic.com, accessed 12 November 2017.

41 See www.diffuser.fm, 23 February 2017.

42 See www.louielouie.net, accessed 26 September 2017.

43 Kyle MacNeill, 'The Reign in Spain: The Best New Bands from the Land of the Setting Sun', www.diymag.com, 4 March 2015.

44 'The Incredible Staggers', www.facebook.com, accessed 24 November 2017.

45 See www.thejackets.ch, accessed 17 November 2017.

46 Quoted in Been, '10 Years after The White Stripes "Saved" It'.

47 Sasha Raspopina, 'Rough and Ready: Behind the Cassette Craze of St Petersburg's Garage-Rock Scene', www.calvertjournal.com, 29 January 2016.

48 Ibid.

Select Bibliography

Altschuler, Glenn C., *All Shook Up: How Rock 'n' Roll Changed America* (New York, 2004)

Anscombe, Isabelle, and Dike Blair, *Punk: Punk Rock/Punk Style/Punk Stance/Punk People/Punk Stars/That Head the New Wave in England and America* (New York, 1978)

Bacon, Tony, *Echo and Twang: Classic Guitar Music* (San Francisco, CA, 1996)

Bangs, Lester, *Psychotic Reactions and Carburetor Dung*, ed. Greil Marcus (New York, 1988)

Barin-Turica, and Stehan Kery, Booklet, *Thai Beat A Go-Go: Volume 1*, Subliminal Sounds SUBCD 11, 2004, compact disc

Bartels, Jim, 'Lenny & The Thundertones', *Kicks*, 7 (1992), p. 72

Been, Eric, '10 Years after The White Stripes "Saved" It, Rock is Again in Crisis', www.theatlantic.com, 5 July 2011

Blair, John, 'Dick Dale: The Man Who Invented Surf Music', *Bomp! 2: Born in the Garage*, ed. Suzy Shaw and Mike Stax (n.p., UT Publishing, 2009), p. 213

Blecha, Peter, 'Etiquette Rules! The Northwest's Reigning '60s Garage-Rock Record Company', www.historylink.org, accessed 19 July 2015

——, 'The Godfather of Northwest Rock and the King of Seattle R&B', www.greenmonkeyrecords.com, January 2006

——, *Sonic Boom: The History of Northwest Rock, from 'Louie Louie' to 'Smells Like Teen Spirit'* (New York, 2009)

Bovey, Seth, '"Don't Tread on Me": The Ethos of '60s Garage Punk', *Popular Music and Society*, xxix/4 (2006), pp. 451–9

Brasor, Philip, 'The Ventures: Still Rocking After 50 Years', www.japantimes.co.jp/culture, 7 August 2008

Brooks, Katherine, 'Meet Los Saicos, The Peruvian Band Credited with Inventing Punk Rock', www.huffingtonpost.com, 15 August 2013

Bryan, Beverly, 'Please Explain: What is Garage Punk? How a Retrograde Strain of Weird, Fun Punk Stays Alive in the Underground, or: Are You Bored with Animal Collective Yet?', www.mtviggy.com, 4 February 2013

Bungert, Anja, 'The Tiles: Beat an der Saar', *Ugly Things*, 17 (1999), pp. 73–5

Burke, Dave, and Alan Taylor, Booklet, *The Fabulous Wailers: The Original Golden Crest Masters*, Ace Records CDCHD 675, 1998, compact disc

Children of Nuggets: Original Artyfacts from the Second Psychedelic Era, 1976–1996, Booklet, Rhino R2 74639, 2005, boxed set of compact discs

Clayson, Alan, *The Beat Merchants: The Origins, History, Impact and Rock Legacy of the 1960s British Pop Groups* (London, 1995)

Coffee, Rich, 'Thee Fourgiven: It Ain't Pretty Down Here', Booklet, *It Ain't Pretty Down Here*, Dionysus ID1233128, 2006, compact disc

Coleman, James, S., *The Adolescent Society: The Social Life of the Teenager and its Impact on Education* (New York, 1961)

Crowley, Kent, *Surf Beat: Rock'n'Roll's Forgotten Revolution* (New York, 2011)

Dalley, Robert J., *Surfin' Guitars: Instrumental Surf Bands of the Sixties*, 2nd edn (Ann Arbor, MI, 1996)

DeRogatis, Jim, *Kaleidoscope Eyes: Psychedelic Rock from the '60s to the '90s* (Secaucus, NJ, 1996)

Deusner, Stephen, 'Punk Pioneer Lenny Kaye Reflects Back on "The Original Sin of Rock 'n' Roll"', www.salon.com, 29 November 2015

Forte, Dan, Booklet, *Twang Thang: The Duane Eddy Anthology*, Rhino Records R2 71223, 1993, compact disc

Frith, Simon, *Sound Effects: Youth, Leisure, and the Politics of Rock'n'Roll*, 2nd edn (New York, 1981)

Gassen, Timothy, *The Knights of Fuzz: The Garage and Psychedelic Music Explosion, 1980–2000*, Purple Cactus Media Productions PCMP 2001, 2001, CD-ROM

Gillett, Charlie, *The Sound of the City: The Rise of Rock and Roll*, 2nd edn (New York, 1996)

GONN, *Frenzology, 1966–1967: Punks Along the Mississippi*, Booklet, MCCM Records MCCM CD 9601, 1996, compact disc

Hall, Ron, *Playing for a Piece of the Door: A History of Garage and Frat Bands in Memphis, 1960–1975* (Memphis, TN, 2001)

Have 'Twangy' Guitar – Will Travel, Booklet, Jamie/Guyden 4007-2, 1999, compact disc

Hibbard, Don J., and Carol Kaleialoha, *The Role of Rock* (Englewood Cliffs, NJ, 1983)

Hicks, Michael, *Sixties Rock: Garage, Psychedelic, and Other Satisfactions* (Urbana, IL, 1999)

Janck, Wayne, and Tad Lathrop, *Cult Rockers* (New York, 1995)

Johnson, Ann, and Mike Stax, 'From Psychotic to Psychedelic: The Garage Contribution to Psychedelia', *Popular Music and Society*, XXIX/4 (2006), pp. 411–25

Joynson, Vernon, *The Acid Trip: A Complete Guide to Psychedelic Music* (Todmorden, 1984)

——, *Fuzz, Acid and Flowers Revisited: A Comprehensive Guide to American Garage, Psychedelic and Hippie Rock, 1964–1975* (London, 2007)

Kaye, Lenny, Liner Notes, *Nuggets: Original Artyfacts from the First Psychedelic Era, 1965–1968*, Elektra 7E 2006, 1972, vinyl LP

Kessler, Gregor, 'The Loosers: Krauts on the Loose', *Ugly Things*, 37 (2014), pp. 139–41

Koda, Cub, Booklet, *Rock Instrumental Classics, Volume 1: The Fifties*, Rhino Records R2 71601, 1994, compact disc

Laing, Dave, *One Chord Wonders: Power and Meaning in Punk Rock* (Oakland, CA, 2015)

Larner, Jeremy, 'What Do They Get from Rock-'n'-Roll?', *Atlantic Monthly*, CCXIV/2 (1964), pp. 44–9

Long, Pat, 'The Psycho Five', in *Shindig! Presents Psychotic Reaction: The U.S. '60s Garage Explosion,* ed. Andy Morten and Jon 'Mojo' Mills (Maidenhead, 2009), pp. 12–19

Lucchini, Massimo, *Nuggetsmania: A Guide to the CD Compilations* (Florence, 2000)

Lundborg, Patrick, with Aaron Milenski and Ron Moore, *The Acid Archives: A Guide to Underground Sounds, 1965–1982* (n.p., 2006)

McIntyre, Iain, 'Chants R&B: Live Witchdoctors', *Ugly Things*, 19 (2001), pp. 49–51

MacNeill, Kyle, 'The Reign in Spain: The Best New Bands from the Land of the Setting Sun', www.diymag.com, 4 March 2015

Markesich, Mark, *TeenBeat Mayhem! Commemorating America's Forgotten Musical Heritage: Those Teenage Rock and Roll Combos of the Swingin' 1960s* (Branford, CT, 2012)

Marsh, Dave, *Louie Louie* (New York, 1993)

Mendoza, Fidel Gutierrez, 'Wildmen in the City: A Story About Los Saicos', Booklet, *Los Saicos: ¡Demolicion! The Complete Recordings,* Munster Records Distolux SL, 2010, compact disc

Miller, Billy, 'The Papa Oom Mow Mow Whoa Dad Bird Dance Beat of The Trashmen', *Kicks*, 7 (1992), pp. 6–16

——, 'Billy Talks with Mike Waggoner and the Bops', *Kicks*, 7 (1992), p. 17

Mills, Jon 'Mojo', and Andy Morten, eds, *Shindig! Annual Number Three* (Maidenhead, n.d.)

Morris, Chris, 'Rock 'n' Roll and Its Discontents', Booklet, *No Thanks! The '70s Punk Rebellion*, Rhino R2 73926, 2003, boxed set of compact discs

Morten, Andy, and Jon 'Mojo' Mills, eds, *Shindig! Presents Psychotic Reaction: The US '60s Garage Explosion* (Maidenhead, n.d.)

Mühl, Otto, 'The Black Lips Want to Get You Drunk', www.anthemmagazine.com, 1 May 2007

Nuggets: Original Artyfacts from the First Psychedelic Era, 1965–1968, Booklet, Rhino R2 75466, 1998, boxed set of compact discs

Oldsberg, Jim, '"Ad Libbing" with The Galaxies', *Lost and Found*, 2 (1993), pp. 89–97

—, 'The Fabulous Jades', *Lost and Found*, 2 (1993), pp. 4–10

—, 'Minnetonka's Abominable Snowmen: The Yetti-Men', *Lost and Found*, 2 (1993), pp. 74–8

Palao, Alec, Booklet, *The Fabulous Wailers: At the Castle | & Co.*, Ace Records CDWIKD 228, 2003, compact disc

Pareles, Jon, 'The Monks' Moment, Recaptured', www.nytimes.com, 8 November 1999

Parypa, Larry, Liner Notes, *This is . . . The Savage Young Sonics*, Norton Records NW 909, 2001, vinyl LP

Pereira, Joseph, 'The Checkmates', *Ugly Things*, 23 (2005), pp. 85–9

—, 'The Quests', *Ugly Things*, 21 (2003), pp. 67–74

—, 'The Straydogs', *Ugly Things*, 19 (2001), pp. 115–17

Pewter, Jim, Booklet, *Dick Dale and His Del-Tones: Greatest Hits, 1961–1976*, GNP Crescendo Records GNPD 2095, 1992, compact disc

Prellberg, Mark, 'Rockin' 'Round the Valley – The '60s Fox Cities Scene', *Lost and Found*, 2 (1993), pp. 37–46

Priore, Domenic, *Riot on Sunset Strip: Rock'n'Roll's Last Stand in Hollywood* (London, 2007)

—, 'The Tall Cool Tale of Paul Revere and the Raiders: A Conversation with Mark Lindsay and Paul Revere', www.sundazed.com, 24 March 2011

Raspopina, Sasha, 'Rough and Ready: Behind the Cassette Craze of St Petersburg's Garage-Rock Scene', www.calvertjournal.com, 29 January 2016

Roller, Peter, *Milwaukee Garage Bands: Generations of Grassroots Rock* (Charleston, SC, 2013)

Rosen, Steven, 'Might the Sonics Be the Great American Rock Band?', www.huffingtonpost.com, accessed 2 March 2016

Savage, Jon, and Stuart Baker, Booklet, *Punk 45: Sick on You! One Way Spit! After the Love and before the Revolution, Vol. 3: Proto-Punk, 1969–76*, Soul Jazz Records SJR CD279, 2014, compact disc

Scheelings, Pim, 'The Motions . . . in Motion', *Ugly Things*, 36 (2013), pp. 35–8

—, *Q65* (n.p., UT Publishing, 2010)

Schmidt, Andrew, 'Andy James: The Missing Link', *Ugly Things*, 17 (1999), pp. 28–31

Schneider, Martin, 'If Peru's Los Saicos Aren't the First Punk Band, They're Pretty Close', www.dangerousminds.net, 26 August 2013

Shaw, Greg, 'The Birth of Surf', *Bomp! 2: Born in the Garage*, ed. Mike Stax and Suzy Shaw (n.p., UT Publishing, 2009), p. 212

—, In Defense of Rock Theory', *BOMP! Saving the World One Record at a Time*, ed. Suzy and Mick Farren (n.p., AMMO Books, 2007), pp. 186–8.

—, 'Prelude to the Morning of an Inventory of the '60s', *Who Put the Bomp*, 6 (1971), p. 9

—, '"Sic Transit Gloria . . .": The Story of Punk Rock in the '60s', Booklet, *Nuggets: Original Artyfacts from the First Psychedelic Era, 1965–1968*, Rhino R2 75466, 1998, boxed set of compact discs, pp. 17–22

—, 'The Vanda-Young Story', in *Bomp! 2: Born in the Garage*, ed. Mike Stax and Suzy Shaw (n.p., UT Publishing, 2009), pp. 284–90

—, and Mick Farren (n.p., AMMO Books, 2007), pp. 186–8

Shaw, Greg, and Lennart Persson, 'Sounds of the Sixties: Part Four: Sweden', in *BOMP! 2: Born in the Garage, ed. Mike Stax and Suzy Shaw* (n.p., UT Publishing, 2009), pp. 270–74

Shaw, Suzy, and Mick Farren, eds, *BOMP! Saving the World One Record at a Time* (n.p., AMMO Books, 2007)

Shaw, Suzy, and Mike Stax, eds, *BOMP! 2: Born in the Garage* (n.p., UT Publishing, 2009)

Smith, Chris, *101 Albums that Changed Popular Music* (New York, 2009)

Sorge, Claudio, 'Ravin' Rokes', *Kicks*, 1 (1979), pp. 47–50

Stax, Anja, 'The Pleasure Seekers', *Ugly Things*, 31 (2011), pp. 55–62

Stax, Mike, Booklet, *Black Monk Time*, Infinite Zero 9 43112-2, 1997, compact disc

—, 'The Dandy Girls, Part 1: Teenage Girl-next-door Rock 'n' Roll', *Ugly Things*, 27 (2008), pp. 163–7

—, 'Danish Beat: Cool Like Frost', *Ugly Things*, 22 (2004), pp. 192–3

—, 'I Joined the Voxx Rebellion and I Didn't Even Get a Lousy T-shirt', in *Bomp! Saving the World One Record at a Time*, ed. Suzy Shaw and Mick Farren (n.p., AMMO Books, 2007), pp. 258–61

——, 'The Life I Live: Q65, The Outsiders, and the Dutch Beat Revolution', *Ugly Things*, 45 (2017), pp. 7–27

——, 'The Masters Apprentices, Part One: Hands of Time', *Ugly Things*, 29 (2009), pp. 13–40

——, 'The Masters Apprentices, Part Two: Band Moll Paradise', *Ugly Things*, 30 (2010), pp. 89–109

——, 'Optical Sound: The Technicolor Tales behind the Numerous Nuggets', Booklet, *Nuggets: Original Artyfacts from the First Psychedelic Era, 1965–1968*, Rhino R2 75466, 1998, boxed set of compact discs

——, with Thor G. Norås, 'The Dandy Girls, Part 2: Guitars, Mascara, and Napalm', *Ugly Things*, 28 (2009), pp. 65–72

Stratton, Jon, 'Englishing Popular Music in the 1960s', in *Britpop and the English Music Tradition*, ed. Andy Bennett and Jon Stratton (Farnham, 2010), pp. 41–54

Szatmary, David P., *Rockin' in Time: A Social History of Rock-and-Roll*, 6th edn (Upper Saddle River, NJ, 2007)

Taylor, Hugo, 'Speaking of the Speakers', *Ugly Things*, 22 (2004), pp. 106–8

'Teen-age Money Music', *Life*, LX/2 (1966), pp. 102–10, www.books.google.com, accessed 13 July 2015

Terich, Jeff, 'Freedom Rock: The Fuzzbox Liturgy of Ty Segall', www.floodmagazine.com, 20 January 2017

True, Everett, *The White Stripes and the Sound of Mutant Blues* (London, 2004)

Unterberger, Richie, *Unknown Legends of Rock'n'Roll: Psychedelic Unknowns, Mad Geniuses, Punk Pioneers, Lo-fi Mavericks, and More* (San Francisco, CA, 1998)

——, *Urban Spacemen and Wayfaring Strangers: Overlooked Innovators and Eccentric Visionaries of '60s Rock* (San Francisco, CA, 2000)

Waghorne, Terry, 'Pirate Radio in the UK', *BOMP! 2: Born in the Garage*, ed. Mike Stax and Suzy Shaw (n.p., UT Publishing, 2009), pp. 152–3

Watts, Jonathan, and Dan Collyns, 'Where Did Punk Begin? A Cinema in Peru', www.theguardian.com, 14 September 2012

White, George R., *Bo Diddley: Living Legend* (Chessington, 1995)

Wood, Randall, Booklet, *Los Nuggetz: '60s Garage and Psych from Latin America*, RockBeat Records ROC-CD 3073, 2013, boxed set of compact discs

Recommended Listening

Singles

Introduction

Duane Eddy, 'Rebel-Rouser'
Bill Justis, 'Raunchy'
The Wailers, 'Beat Guitar'
Link Wray, 'Rumble'

Chapter One

The Astronauts, 'Firewater'
The Belairs, 'Mr. Moto'
Dick Dale and His Deltones, 'Misirlou'
The Kingsmen, 'Louie Louie'
The Sonics, 'Strychnine'
The Trashmen, 'Surfin' Bird'

Chapter Two

Randy Alvey and the Green Fuz, 'Green Fuz'
The Blox, 'Hangin' Out'
Bohemian Vendetta, 'Enough'
The Bourbons, 'Of Old Approximately'
Children of the Mushroom, 'You Can't Erase a Mirror'
The Chocolate Watchband, 'Sweet Young Thing'
Count Five, 'Psychotic Reaction'
The Electric Prunes, 'I Had Too Much to Dream (Last Night)'
The Grim Reepers, 'Two Souls'
Half-Pint and the Fifths, 'Orphan Boy'
The Human Expression, 'Optical Sound'
The Illusions, 'City of People'

The Invasion, 'Do You Like What You See?'
The Lavender Hour, 'I've Got a Way with Girls'
The Magic Plants, 'I'm a Nothing'
Nobody's Children, 'Good Times'
Paul Revere and the Raiders, 'Hungry'
The Savages, 'The World Ain't Round It's Square'
The Shades of Night, 'Fluctuation'
The Sound Barrier, 'Hey, Hey'
The Sparkles, 'I Want to Be Free'
The Dave Starkey Five, 'Stand There'
The Stoics, 'Enough of What I Need'
The Syndicate of Sound, 'Little Girl'
The Third Bardo, 'I'm Five Years Ahead of My Time'
The 13th Floor Elevators, 'You're Gonna Miss Me'

Chapter Three

The Boots (Germany), 'Gaby'
The Bunnys (Japan), 'Moanin''
The Cat (Thailand), 'Do the Watusi'
The Masters Apprentices (Australia), 'Undecided'
The Missing Links (Australia), 'Wild About You'
The Monks (Germany), 'I Hate You'
The Outsiders (The Netherlands), 'Thinking About Today'
Q65 (The Netherlands), 'The Life I Live'
The Rattles (Germany), 'Betty Jean'
The Rokes (UK/Italy), 'She Asks of You'
Los Shain's (Peru), 'Shain's A Go Go'
Them (UK), 'Gloria'
Tom Thumb (New Zealand), 'I Need You'

Chapter Four

The Cramps, 'Garbageman'
New York Dolls, 'Bad Girl'
The Stooges, 'No Fun'
Suicide, 'Ghost Rider'
Up, 'Just Like an Aborigine'

Chapter Five

The Barracudas (UK), '(I Wish it Could Be) 1965 Again'
The Chesterfield Kings, 'Fluctuation'
Creatures of the Golden Dawn, 'Same All Over the World'
The Gravedigger Five, 'Spooky'
The Nomads (Sweden), 'Where the Wolf Bane Blooms'
The Original Sins, 'Feel'
The Pandoras, 'Hot Generation'

Chapter Six

Black Lips, 'Throw It Away'
The Gories, 'Feral'
The Jackets (Switzerland), 'Don't Turn Yourself In'
The Incredible Staggers (Austria), 'The Zombies of Love'
The Mummies, 'In and Out'
The Sloths, 'Makin' Love'
The White Stripes, 'Seven Nation Army'

Recommended Compilations and Compilation Series

Acid Visions (Voxx LP, 1983)
Back from the Grave (Crypt CD, vols 1–10, 2010–15)
Bad Vibrations (Fossil Records LP, no date)
Boulders (Moxie LP, vols 1–11, 1980–199?)
The Chosen Few (A-Go-Go/Tom Tom LP, vols 1–2, 1982–3)
The Cicadelic 60's (Cicadelic LP/CD, 1983–98)
Ear-piercing Punk (Trash LP, 1979) (AIP CD, 1996)
Essential Pebbles (AIP CD, vols 1–3, AIP, 1997–2000)
Filling the Gap (Past & Present CD, 2004)
Fuzz, Flaykes, & Shakes (Dionysus CD, vols 1–7, 1999–2002)
Garage Beat '66 (Sundazed CD, vols 1–7, 2004–7)
Garage Sale: 19 Wyld and Savage Bands! (ROIR Cassette, 1985)
Get Off My Back (Norton LP, 2009)
Girls in the Garage (Romulan LP, vols 1–8, 1987–98)
Gravel (Kumquat May CD, vols 1–5, c. 2005)
Green Crystal Ties (Cicadelic CD, vols 1–10, 1998)
Highs in the Mid-sixties (AIP LP, vols 1–23, 1983–6)
The Human Expression & Other Psychedelic Groups (Collectables CD, 1998)

I Wanna Come Back from the World of LSD (Cicadelic CD, 1999)
I've Had Enough (Norton LP, 2009)
Last of the Garage Punk Unknowns (Crypt CD, vols 1–8, 2015–16)
Louisiana Punk (Eva CD, 2008)
Mindrocker (Past & Present CD, vols 1–13, 2002)
Nuggets (Rhino LP, vols 1–12, 1984–198?)
Nuggets: Original Artyfacts from the First Psychedelic Era, 1965–1968
(Elektra LP, 1972; Rhino CD, 1998)
Off the Wall (Past & Present CD, vols 1–2, 2009)
Pebbles (BFD LP, vols 1–10, 1979–80)
Pebbles (AIP CD, vols 1–9, 1992–6)
Pebbles (AIP LP, vols 11–22, 1983–7)
Psychedelic Unknowns (Calico/Scrap! LP/CD, vols 1–11, 1979–199?)
Quagmire (Finest Hour CD, vols 1–8, n.d.)
The Quill Records Story: The Best of Chicago Garage Bands
(Collectables CD, 1997)
Rough Diamonds: The History of Garage Band Music (Voxx LP, vol. 6, 1984)
Scum of the Earth (Sound Stories CD, vols 1–2, 1998)
She Was So Bad (Norton LP, 2009)
Sixties Rebellion (WayBack Records, vols 1–16, 1993–2009)
Teen Blast USA! (Gyro CD, vols 1–2, 1995)
Teenage Shutdown (Crypt LP/CD, vols 1–15, 1998–2000)
Texas Flashbacks (Psychic Circle CD, vols 1–6, 2010)
Texas Punk (Cicadelic LP, vols 1–10, 1984–7)
Three O'Clock Merrian Webster Time (Cicadelic LP/CD, 1982/2011)
Trip in Tyme (Manic Mustang CD, vols 1–5, n.d.)
Vile Vinyl (Past & Present CD, 2009)
What a Way to Die (Satan LP, 1983)
Worldbeaters (Krazy World CD, vols 1–11, n.d.)
You Gotta Have . . . Moxie (AIP/Moxie CD, vols 1–2, 1998–9)
You Tore My Brain (Norton LP, 2010)

Online Resources

www.beyondthebeatgeneration.com
Everett True's Australian Garage Rock Primer, www.collapseboard.com
Fancy: Fashion, Art and Crap, www.fancymag.com
www.garagehangover.com
www.garagesector.blogspot.com
www.mza-garage.blogspot.com
www.nederbiet.nl
New Zealand Music of the 60's, 70's and a Bit of 80's,
 www.sergent.com.au/music
www.paradiseofgaragecomps.blogspot.com
'The 60s Popular Music Scene in the Far East'
 www.questing.wordpress.com
www.psychedelicbabymag.com
Radiodiffusion Internasionaal Annexe,
 www.radiodiffusion.wordpress.com
www.shindig-magazine.com
www.southerngaragebands.com
www.ugly-things.com
'The Uruguayan Invasion', www.uruguaynow.com
'Weird Psychedelic Soundwaves from Southeast Asia in the 60s and 70s',
 www.rateyourmusic.com/list/novocaine69

Acknowledgements

The idea for this book first came from John Scanlan, editor of the Reverb Series for Reaktion Books. John contacted me and encouraged me to write a proposal for a book on the subject of garage rock, and I am deeply grateful for his invitation to do so. Since then, he has guided me through the process of creating a book with unfailing professionalism, cheerfully answering my many questions and offering me sensible advice.

I would also like to thank several administrators at my home institution for their support. Dr Guiyou Huang, Chancellor of LSU Alexandria, and Dr Barbara Hatfield, Vice Chancellor for Academic Affairs, helped me tremendously by approving my request for sabbatical leave; being free of my usual duties for a semester gave me the time I needed to finish this book and to make it better than it would have been otherwise. I am also grateful for the unflagging support of Dr Holly Wilson, Chair of Arts, English and Humanities, who has been an advocate for this project ever since it came to be.

Above all, I am grateful to my wife Sherry for exposing me to '60s garage rock in the first place. She helped me to realize in the 1980s that garage rock is worth listening to, no matter how crude or inept it may seem. She also gave me invaluable assistance on this project, finding research materials for me, buying recordings and fanzines that I wouldn't have bought on my own and teaching me how to use various functions on the computer to perform much-needed tasks. Her help has made the writing of this book much easier.

Photo Acknowledgements

The author and the publishers wish to express their thanks to the below sources of illustrative material and/or permission to reproduce it.

Author's collection: pp. 6, 9, 11, 21, 24, 26, 32, 39, 52, 86, 89, 96, 104, 128, 131, 132, 135, 141, 144, 146, 147, 149, 153, 165, 166, 172; Courtesy John Broven, Golden Crest Records Collection at the Library of Congress: p. 18; Mike Dillon: p. 69; Donutte: p. 175: Getty Images: p. 37 (Michael Ochs Archives); Michael Morel: p. 167; National Archives of the Netherlands (Nationaal Archief): p. 122; ThomasFHH: p. 106.

Index

Page numbers in *italics* refer to illustrations